Presented To:

_____

From:

_____

Date:

_____

Understanding
BIBLE
Mysteries

DESTINY IMAGE BOOKS BY IRA L. MILLIGAN

Understanding the Dreams You Dream, Volume I and II

*Understanding the Dreams You Dream,
Revised and Expanded*

*The Ultimate Guide to Understanding
the Dreams You Dream*

Rightly Dividing the Word

The Scorpion Within

Understanding
BIBLE
Mysteries

Examining 13 Christian Myths and Half Truths

IRA L. MILLIGAN

DESTINY IMAGE® PUBLISHERS, INC.
P.O. Box 310, Shippensburg, PA 17257-0310
"Promoting Inspired Lives."

This book and all other Destiny Image, Revival Press, MercyPlace, Fresh Bread, Destiny Image Fiction, and Treasure House books are available at Christian bookstores and distributors worldwide.

For a U.S. bookstore nearest you, call 1-800-722-6774.
For more information on foreign distributors, call 717-532-3040.
Reach us on the Internet: www.destinyimage.com.

Previously published as *Truth or Consequences* ISBN 0-97023-756-1

ISBN 13 TP: 978-0-7684-0296-4
ISBN 13 Ebook: 978-0-7684-8793-0

For Worldwide Distribution, Printed in the U.S.A.

1 2 3 4 5 6 7 8 / 16 15 14 13 12

DEDICATION

This book is dedicated to the modern Bereans—those faithful, dedicated saints of God who, like the noble converts in Acts 17:10-11, *"received the word with all readiness, and searched the Scriptures daily to find out whether these things were so."*

APPRECIATION

I wish to express my heartfelt thanks to those precious saints of God who have supported us with their prayers and substance to allow us to give ourselves wholly to prayer and to the ministry of the Word. Special thanks go to my wife Judy, and my friends Jimmy and Chris for proofreading the manuscript.

Jesus said to him, "I am the way, the truth, and the life. No one comes to the Father except through Me"
(John 14:6).

CONTENTS

Introduction
 IS THE GLASS HALF FULL OR
 HALF EMPTY? 15

Chapter One
 TO TITHE, OR NOT TO TITHE? 19

Chapter Two
 THE RAPTURE QUESTION 37

Chapter Three
 POSITIVE CONFESSION 59

Chapter Four
 FIRE INSURANCE 73

Chapter Five
 THE MYSTERY OF GODLINESS 87

Chapter Six
 THE MYSTERY OF BAPTISMS 103

Chapter Seven
 THE MYSTERY OF THE BRIDE 119

Chapter Eight
   SIN, SICKNESS,
   AND CHASTISEMENT 133

Chapter Nine
   THE LAW OF JEALOUSY 147

Chapter Ten
   UNANSWERED PRAYER 163

Chapter Eleven
   TO BIND A STRONG MAN 179

Chapter Twelve
   THE BELIEVER'S PRIESTHOOD 193

Chapter Thirteen
   CUTTING CORNERS 207

IS THE GLASS HALF FULL OR HALF EMPTY?

Although truth is an absolute—meaning it isn't relative—truth's application is not. Truth's application is always relative to its context. For instance, probably everyone has toyed with the rhetorical question, is the glass half full or half empty? There is no actual answer. If the glass was empty and you are filling the glass, then at midpoint it is half full. If the glass was full and you are drinking from it, then at some point it is half empty. In other words, if there is a correct answer it is only correct relative to one's specific action or viewpoint.

Many theological questions have to be approached the same way. Truth is an absolute, but the interpretation of truth varies with each individual application. If the biblical writers' actions and viewpoints aren't taken into consideration when interpreting Scripture, error will often be the result. Heresy usually arises from misapplication (i.e., taking things out of their proper context), not necessarily from malicious intent. Nevertheless, selfish motives often lie behind much of the erroneous application of Scripture present in the Christian church today.

A wise Christian historian once observed that every major heresy began as a minor deviation from the truth. But we must ask the question, what caused the deviation? And, what is its eventual consequence? Though the consequence of a doctrinal error may seem minor in its beginning, its true ability to blind and bind is only revealed when it is magnified by time and sustained by tradition.

In Ephesians 4:14, Paul admonished the saints:

Be no more children, tossed to and fro, and carried about with every wind of doctrine, by the sleight of men, and cunning craftiness, whereby they lie in wait to deceive (KJV).

But in many churches this warning has fallen upon deaf ears. Not only has the Church been tossed to and fro like a derelict ship on stormy waters, but crafty pirates have boarded her weathered decks and rifled her treasures with such precision and skill that their theft has often gone virtually undetected.

Besides Paul, Peter is another who warned the saints of these marauders long before they came aboard:

But there were false prophets also among the people, even as there shall be false teachers among you, who privily shall bring in damnable heresies, even denying the Lord that bought them, and bring upon themselves swift destruction. And many shall follow their pernicious ways; by reason of whom the way of truth shall be evil spoken of. And through covetousness shall they with feigned words make merchandise of you... (2 Peter 2:1-3 KJV).

Their deceptive heresies have made inroads into almost every doctrine known to the Church, yet these clever pirates are often applauded as heralds of truth and righteousness. Their "camps" are many and diverse, yet they have one thing in common—they all use the Word of God for personal gain and fame. As Peter said, *"While they promise* [the saints] *liberty, they themselves are the servants of corruption..."* (2 Peter 2:19 KJV). By making promises in God's name that He has not made, and that He does not have any intention of ever fulfilling, they deceive the simple and exploit the innocent for their own personal gain.

Mingling with God's true apostles and taking advantage of the restoration of this important ministry, often these "deceitful workers" zealously "transform themselves into apostles of Christ" and seize the moment, capitalizing upon the expectancy of the faithful to rob them of every precious thing Christ has purchased for them (see 2 Corinthians 11:13). Sadly, many saints embrace these deceivers' deception and even go so far as to defend them when their heresies are confronted and denounced.

Although God's Word affords us *"all things that pertain to life and godliness,"* nevertheless, because of apathy and ignorance, many of His people are destroyed for lack of knowledge (see 2 Peter 1:3; Hosea 4:6). This book exposes several of these deceptive doctrines and their serious—sometimes even deadly—consequences.

It's time to fall in love with Jesus all over again, saints. He is still *"the* [only] *way, the **truth**, and the life"* (John 14:6). Let the modern Bereans arise!

> *"Bring all the tithes into the storehouse, that there may be food in My house, and try Me now in this,"* says the Lord of hosts, *"if I will not open for you the windows of heaven and pour out for you such blessing that there will not be room enough to receive it"* (Malachi 3:10).

Chapter One

TO TITHE, OR NOT TO TITHE?

Many Christians believe the Church is precariously close to experiencing another reformation. As Wolfgang Simson aptly pointed out in his excellent book, *Houses That Change the World*, it has experienced two thus far: In the sixteenth century Luther's teachings started a reformation of *doctrine*. And two centuries later, Wesley's teachings on sanctification and holiness (followed by the outpouring of the Holy Spirit that began in 1901) brought about a reformation of *spirituality*. Simson concludes what we now need is a reformation of *structure*. I agree.

Of necessity, as Luther stoutly proclaimed, the battle cry of all true reformers is *"solo scriptura."* But herein lies the rub—it's not always easy to agree on exactly what the Scriptures teach and mean on some subjects. To avoid error during transitional times like these, it is absolutely essential for everyone to carefully follow proper rules of biblical interpretation, especially when formulating doctrine.

One common mistake made by some modern theologians is to assume that if the New Testament is silent on a subject introduced in the Old Testament, then that subject is no longer applicable today. Because it isn't mentioned, they say it has been "done away with." This type of error is called establishing doctrine through *absence of mention*.

"Absence of mention" is the reason some churches shun musical instruments during worship. In spite of numerous passages showing that tambourines and various stringed instruments were commonly used during worship in the Old Testament, they aren't mentioned in the New Testament at all. The majority of churches use them anyway of course. It is apparent that God never intended otherwise.

Another example of using absence of mention to incorrectly establish doctrine is when some teach against tithing by claiming, "The apostles didn't pay tithes." It is true the Bible does not mention them paying tithes, but it doesn't mention them using musical instruments either—and they probably did. Although there is no way of knowing for certain whether they played musical instruments, we *can* be sure they paid tithes. The biblical evidence proves it.

How do we know the apostles paid tithes? For one reason, all the apostles were Jews. Years after the initial outpouring of the Holy Spirit, Paul returned to Jerusalem, and James and the elders testified, *"You see, brother, how many myriads of Jews there are who have believed; and they are **all zealous for the law**"* (Acts 21:18-21). Because tithing was contained within the Law, it is obvious the apostles continued paying tithes long after they were saved and filled with the Holy Spirit.

IS TITHING FOR TODAY?

I was reading a book recently and came across a chapter on tithing—or on *not* tithing, I should say. Now this particular author is on the cutting edge of what God is doing when he writes about such things as house churches and how the apostolic ministry functions in conjunction with them, but I think some of the things he has written against church government and tithing go over the edge. I think his "anti-establishment" mentality has led him to cast out the baby with the bathwater on more than one of these subjects. To discover the whole truth on tithing we need to ask, as Paul would, *"What saith the scripture?"* (Galatians 4:30 KJV).

This author's first argument against tithing said that because tithing is in the Law of Moses, it isn't for today—but is that true? If something is in the Law, does that automatically mean that it isn't relevant today and that it is not to be observed anymore? The Law commands us to honor our fathers and mothers, and no one contends that we shouldn't honor them because *that* commandment is in the Law (see Ephesians 6:2). There are numerous other commandments that we still keep as well, so that is not a valid reason to refuse to pay tithes (for example, take a look at the list in Mark 10:19). If we are sincere about wanting to please God, we need to examine the Scriptures carefully and see what they really have to say about this doctrine.

First, as everyone agrees, the Scriptures show that Abraham paid tithes to Melchizedek (who was a type of Christ) long before the Law was given (see Hebrews 7:1-4,17). But here the argument contends that even though Abraham did pay tithes, he only paid them once, and then only on the spoils of war—but the scriptural evidence shows otherwise!

God said:

I know him [Abraham], *that he will command his children and his household after him, and they shall keep the way of the Lord, to do justice and judgment; that the Lord may bring upon Abraham that which he hath spoken of him* (Genesis 18:19 KJV).

So, according to God's own testimony, we should be able to see Abraham's practices reflected in his children's conduct—and we do. The Bible records that Jacob also paid tithes, not only on the spoils of war, but on everything he earned! Jacob promised God, *"...And of all that You give me I will surely give a tenth to You"* (Genesis 28:22). Thus, the Scriptures clearly show tithing was the norm for Abraham and his family, and, we might add, as Christians we are supposed to walk in the steps of faithful Abraham! (See Romans 4:12.)

But some object with, "But that's all Old Testament stuff. Jesus didn't condone tithing"—or did He? Jesus said:

Woe unto you, scribes and Pharisees, hypocrites! for you **pay tithe** *of mint and anise and cummin, and have omitted the weightier matters of the law, judgment, mercy, and faith:* **these ought ye to have done**, *and not to leave the other undone* (Matthew 23:23 KJV).

If we are not supposed to pay tithes, why did Jesus say that we should? Some would answer, "Jesus was rebuking them under the Law. That all changed after He died." But is that right? Not according to the Gospel writers! Luke said, *"The law and the prophets were until John. Since that time the kingdom of God has been preached..."* (Luke 16:16).

The Law ended with John the Baptist and grace started when Jesus came on the scene. The apostle John wrote, *"For the law was given through Moses, but grace and truth came through Jesus Christ"* (John 1:17). Jesus is the same yesterday, today, and forever. His message never changes either. He taught nothing but Kingdom principles while He was here on earth, as even a casual examination of His teachings confirm. For example, when Jesus began His ministry, Mark quotes Him as saying, *"...The time is fulfilled, and the kingdom of God is at hand: repent ye, and believe the gospel"* (Mark 1:15 KJV). As the two verses below show, Matthew's Gospel reveals the same thing:

> *You have heard that it was said by them of old time* [in the Law of Moses], *thou shalt not commit adultery: But I say unto you, that whosoever looks on a woman to lust after her has committed adultery with her already in his heart* (Matthew 5:27-28 KJV).

> *You have heard that it was said, "An eye for an eye and a tooth for a tooth." But I tell you not to resist an evil person. But whoever slaps you on your right cheek, turn the other to him also* (Matthew 5:38-39).

As one can see from these sample verses, Jesus's teachings emphasized grace and true holiness, not Law and legalism. But, as we saw in Matthew 23:23, His teachings did include tithing, as the parallel passage in Luke 11:42 also affirms:

But woe to you Pharisees! **For you tithe** *mint and rue and all manner of herbs, and pass by justice and the love of God.* **These you ought to have done,** *without leaving the others undone.*

And finally, in reference to tithing and the Law, James's verdict in Acts chapter 15 is often quoted as the final authority for rejecting the doctrine of tithing. James wrote:

For it seemed good to the Holy Spirit, and to us, to lay upon you no greater burden than these necessary things: that you abstain from things offered to idols, from blood, from things strangled, and from sexual immorality. If you keep yourselves from these, you will do well (Acts 15:28-29).

The argument goes something like this: "Because James didn't mention tithing when he summed up the essential parts of the Law that are still applicable under grace, Gentiles aren't required to pay tithes." The problem with this reasoning is that James's verdict was in direct reference to certain misguided brethren from Jerusalem who were teaching the brethren, *"…Unless you are circumcised according to the custom of Moses,* **you cannot be saved"** (Acts 15:1).

James's verdict only addressed matters of salvation! Tithing is *not* a matter of salvation; it is a matter of obtaining God's promised blessings through obedience to His will (more on that later). Because tithing is contained *in* the Law doesn't mean it is *of* the Law. Tithing was before the Law, contained within the Law, and sanctioned by Jesus after the Law. As we have mentioned before, honoring one's parents is also in the Law, but that doesn't annul its importance under grace. Tithing has been an essential part of God's financial plan to support His army and workforce from the beginning. His plan hasn't changed. Paul asked:

> *Who ever goes to war at his own expense? Who plants a vineyard and does not eat of its fruit? Or who tends a flock and does not drink of the milk of the flock? Do I say these things as a mere man? Or does not the law say the same also? For it is written in the law of Moses, "You shall not muzzle an ox while it treads out the grain...."*

> *If we have sown spiritual things for you, is it a great thing if we reap your material things?* (1 Corinthians 9:7-9,11)

IS TITHING VOLUNTARY OR MANDATORY?

Another objection often put forth by the naysayers is, "Since we are under grace, and tithing, unlike freewill offerings, is considered obligatory, it is wrong to pay tithes." Again, we must ask ourselves what the Scriptures have to say about this. After all, most of us agree that they, and they alone, are the final authority in all such matters!

Although Paul didn't directly address the doctrine of tithing, he did address obligatory giving in his letter to the Romans. He explained that the reason he was going to Jerusalem was to deliver a special offering the saints from Macedonia and Achaia had taken up:

*For it pleased those from Macedonia and Achaia to make a certain contribution for the poor among the saints who are in Jerusalem. It pleased them indeed, and they are their **debtors**. For if the Gentiles have been partakers of their spiritual things, their **duty** is also to minister to them in material things* (Romans 15:26-27).

The teaching that because we are under grace we can do anything we want to do and we are answerable to no one is taking liberty to extremes. Paul cautioned the Galatians, *"For, brethren, ye have been called unto liberty; only use not liberty for an occasion to the flesh, but by love serve one another"* (Galatians 5:13 KJV).

Under grace all submission should be voluntary, so mandatory giving *is* contrary to grace. But giving because we have an obligation to support those who minister to us in spiritual things is not. Paul said, *"Let him who is taught the word share in all good things with him who teaches"* (Galatians 6:6). So the question is not whether we should support those who give themselves *"continually to prayer and to the ministry of the word"* (Acts 6:4), but rather, how much should we give them? The answer is both practical and biblical. We should give them a minimum of 10 percent.

TITHING'S SPECIAL PROMISE

In Second Corinthians 1:20, Paul said all of God's promises are "yes" and "amen" (sure and certain). However, there is one often-quoted promise that God has no intention of fulfilling regardless of the sincerity of those who quote it—not in the way they frame the promise, that is. The promise I'm referring to is a distortion of Malachi 3:10:

> *"Bring all the tithes into the storehouse, that there may be food in My house, and try Me now in this," says the Lord of hosts, "if I will not open for you the windows of heaven and pour out for you such blessing that there will not be room enough to receive it."*

Many pastors teach this scripture is promising abundant financial blessings upon those who faithfully pay their tithes. It is not! Money and natural wealth aren't poured out through the open windows of heaven—but spiritual revelations are! God always puts spiritual things ahead of natural things.

Jesus said, *"If you have not been faithful in the unrighteous mammon, who will commit to your trust the true riches?"* (Luke 16:11). Notice how Jesus contrasts money and true riches in this scripture. Here Jesus teaches the promised return for being faithful in giving isn't more money than we can spend—rather, it is something far greater. In fact, as Malachi said, it is so great that often we don't have enough room to receive all of it!

What are these unsearchable riches? Paul defined heaven's riches as wisdom, knowledge, and *"the full assurance of understanding"* (Colossians 2:2-3). Likewise, Solomon said the proceeds of wisdom are:

> *...better than the profits of silver, and her gain than fine gold. She is more precious than rubies, and all the*

things you may desire cannot compare with her (Proverbs 3:14-15).

In spite of what we may have been told, God does not promise us an abundance of money for being faithful in tithing. He promises spiritual revelation, which leads to an abundance of faith. "Full assurance of understanding" is faith! This world's currency is money. With enough money you can buy whatever the world has to offer, but God's Kingdom operates on faith. There are some things money can't buy, but there's nothing that faith can't obtain!

You may be asking, "But didn't God promise natural provision too?" Of course He did, but He didn't promise more than you have room for! Jesus said:

> *Now if God so clothes the grass of the field...will He not much more clothe you, O you of little faith? Therefore do not worry, saying, "What shall we eat?" or "What shall we drink?" or "What shall we wear?"*
>
> *But seek first the kingdom of God and His righteousness, and all these things shall be added to you* (Matthew 6:30-31,33).

Malachi went on to promise faithful tithers that God *"...will rebuke the devourer for your sakes, so that he will not destroy the fruit of your ground..."* (Malachi 3:11).

Notice in each of these scriptures that God puts the emphasis on the eternal, spiritual things rather than on the natural, temporal things. So, when paying your tithes, remember to look for God's abundant *spiritual* blessings. He is faithful to fulfill His promises—exactly as He made them. As Isaiah promised:

> *If you are willing and obedient, you shall eat the good of the land; but if you refuse and rebel, you shall be devoured by the sword; for the mouth of the Lord has spoken* (Isaiah 1:19-20).

TITHING'S SYMBOLISM IN SCRIPTURE

Of all the symbols found in the Bible, none intrigue me more than numbers. In *Understanding the Dreams You Dream, Volume II,* I devoted five chapters to the meaning of numbers alone. Although numbers are found in almost every book in the Bible, their meanings are often obscure. The hidden meaning found in tithing is no exception. The word *tithe* literally means a "tenth," and when *ten* is used symbolically it means "to weigh or measure" (to determine whether to accept or reject whatever is being measured). In other words, the number ten means a test or a trial!

For example, in Revelation 2:10 God warned the church in Smyrna:

> *Do not fear any of those things which you are about to suffer. Indeed, the devil is about to throw some of you into prison, that you may be tested, and you will have tribulation ten days. Be faithful until death, and I will give you the crown of life.*

The "ten days" of tribulation God warned them about was certainly symbolic (as all of Revelation is) because in reality, history records that the early church endured persecution for over two hundred years!

God tested their faithfulness. That's what tithes and offerings are all about. Every time God gives us something, He tests us to see where our heart is. Jesus said, *"Give alms of such things as you have; then indeed all things are clean to you"* (Luke 11:41). God's motivation for asking for tithes and offerings isn't selfishness; it's assurance. He wants our hearts pure and free from the power of covetousness. Tithing is God's test to reveal where our hearts are when it comes to handling money.

That's the reason He asks for 10 percent, not 12 or 15. He's weighing us in the balances to see whether we are covetous or whether we love Him with all our hearts. Be careful—guard your hearts, not your wallets. Pay your tithes!

Another number closely associated with tithing in Scripture is *five*. The number ten reveals that tithing is a continual test of our stewardship—it is God's way of seeing if we will be faithful in that which belongs to another (see Luke 16:12). In a similar way, the hidden meaning of the number five shows us what happens if we fail the test.

"If a man wants at all to redeem any of his tithes, he shall add one-fifth to it" (Leviticus 27:31). Some ministers say this scripture means that if you "borrow" your tithes for a season, then you have to add 20 percent to them when you pay them back (and it *does* mean that under the Law). However, the true spiritual meaning is actually much more than that

(remember, "the Law is spiritual"—see Romans 7:14). In Bible numerology, *five* means "work" or "service." In other words, the penalty for not paying tithes is to go into *debt*. Proverbs 22:7 says, *"...The borrower is servant to the lender."*

Although we may be in debt for reasons other than refusing to pay tithes (such as poor financial management or slothfulness), God's promise to faithful tithers to "rebuke the devourer" goes a long way toward helping us prosper and live debt-free lives (see Malachi 3:11).

Many Christians believe they cannot afford to pay their tithes because of their high debt load, not realizing their failure to tithe is one of the reasons they are in debt in the first place! And often the accumulated interest they are paying equals or even exceeds the simple 10 percent that God requires. My personal experience has been that God's ways are always best. Be obedient. *"If you are willing and obedient, you shall eat the good of the land"* (Isaiah 1:19). Why not give tithing a try?

TITHING'S PRIMARY PURPOSE

So far we've discussed several aspects of tithing, including where the custom originated (in Abraham), whether Abraham's descendants paid tithes (Jacob shows us they did), whether we should pay them today (Jesus said we should), how they should be paid (not legalistically but joyfully), why tithing is 10 percent (it is the "test" of our stewardship), what the penalty is for failing the test (we may go into debt), and what the true reward is for tithing (spiritual riches and protection from the devourer). Now we need to examine two more aspects of tithing—how tithes are supposed to be used and who should receive them.

God reveals the purpose for tithing in Malachi 3:10: *"Bring all the tithes into the storehouse, that there may be food in My house…."* Jesus explained the spiritual meaning of food in John 4:34: *"My food is to do the will of Him who sent Me, and to finish His work."* So the purpose of tithing is to enable God's workers to do His will and finish His work. In other words, the stated purpose of tithing is to support the work of the ministry.

TITHING'S RIGHTFUL RECIPIENTS

From this it should be obvious that anyone who is at work about the King's business is a qualified recipient of tithes. The common understanding that tithes should only be paid to pastors isn't scriptural; there are many ministers besides pastors who faithfully preach the gospel. Jesus said, *"He who reaps receives wages, and gathers fruit for eternal life, that both he who sows and he who reaps may rejoice together"* (John 4:36). Whether His ministers are sowing or reaping, they all need support, and God instituted tithes and offerings to do just that. First Corinthians 9:14 says, *"The Lord has commanded that those who preach the gospel should live from the gospel."*

It's interesting that the Holy Spirit inspired Paul to write this verse instead of Peter. Paul chose to support himself by making tents, and some teach that all itinerant ministers should imitate Paul and be self-supported, but the Scriptures teach otherwise.

First, contrary to what many believe and teach, Paul was not fully self-supported. He asked the Corinthians:

Did I commit sin in humbling myself that you might be exalted, because I preached the gospel of God to you free of charge? I robbed other churches, taking wages from them to minister to you (2 Corinthians 11:7-8).

Initially, Paul's missionary work was always without charge, but he freely received tithes and offerings from his converts once they were established in the faith. For example, as the scripture quoted above shows, when Paul founded the Corinthian church he did so "free of charge," refusing to receive any support or help from them whatsoever. But right before his third return visit to them, he revealed the "rule" he operated under concerning giving and receiving:

…but having hope, when your faith is increased, that we shall be enlarged by you according to our rule abundantly, to preach the gospel in the regions beyond you… (2 Corinthians 10:15-16 KJV).

This scripture is explicit. It clearly shows that once the churches were established in the faith, Paul depended upon them for financial support when he sailed into uncharted waters. Otherwise, it would have been impossible for him to accomplish everything he did (also see 1 Corinthians 9:18; Philippians 4:15-16).

Second, there is scriptural evidence of the twelve apostles relying on support from other believers. When confronted with the widows' needs in Acts 6:

The twelve summoned the multitude of the disciples and said, "It is not desirable that we should leave the word of God and serve tables. ...But we will give ourselves continually to prayer and to the ministry of the word" (Acts 6:2,4).

Unfortunately, in spite of God's plan, many of God's workers lack proper support. If tithes were paid faithfully, used properly, and distributed correctly there would be little or no shortage.

QUESTIONS AND ANSWERS

1. Should pastors pay tithes, and if so, to whom?

Yes, pastors, like everyone else, should pay tithes. In fact, the Bible teaches that a church's leaders are responsible to set the example for the rest of the flock (see 1 Timothy 4:12). So the question naturally arises, to whom should they pay them?

Most pastors have someone they look to for spiritual oversight and accountability, so this is one legitimate avenue for giving. Another is giving into missions, both home and abroad. Since the purpose of the tithe is primarily to support ministry, itinerant ministers and missionaries qualify as tithing recipients. A third option is giving a portion of the tithe to the poor, which brings us to the next question.

2. Should tithes be used to support the poor?

The Bible teaches that the church is responsible for the welfare of the orphans and widows within each congregation (see Acts 6; 1 Timothy 5). Because the primary purpose of tithes is to support the work of the ministry, and ministering to the poor is part of the ministry, helping them financially is a legitimate use of tithes.

3. Should we tithe net or gross income?

The Bible shows that tithes should be paid on the "increase" (see Deuteronomy 14:22). Although a business should only tithe on the net—because that is the increase—tithes on personal income should normally be paid on the gross.

4. Should tithes be used to build church buildings?

The answer to this question rests upon whether the church building project in question is of God or not. Because tithes actually belong to God, He can direct their use in any way and anywhere He sees fit. In other words, if the church building is actually ordained of God, then it is part of the work of the ministry; so yes, in that case tithes could be used to build it. Otherwise, no. Even so, the *primary* use of tithes should be to support ministers who are doing the work of the ministry.

5. Is the church the "storehouse" of Malachi 3:10?

Many pastors teach that the storehouse Malachi referred to in Malachi 3:10 *("Bring ye all the tithes into the store-house...")* is the church—and it can be—but it cannot be limited to that single interpretation. The Hebrew word translated *storehouse* simply means "depository" and probably refers to the barns used to hold the produce and animals that, in Malachi's day, were commonly brought to the priests in payment. Today's equivalent would be a bank used by any minister or ministry.

RECOMMENDED READING

Purifying the Altar by Al Houghton (available at www.wordatwork.org). This book explains how the altar sanctifies the gift. A polluted altar defiles the gift. A must-read for all who are interested in the grace of giving.

Chapter Two

THE RAPTURE QUESTION

Several years ago I sat down with a friend in a Mexican restaurant that serves the customary corn chips and dip before the meal. As I reached for a chip, my friend asked, "Are you pre-chip or post-chip?"

Caught completely off guard, I stopped in mid-reach, slightly confused by the question. *Was he asking my views on the timing of the rapture?* I wondered. Catching the glint in his eye, I realized he was jesting, so with raised eyebrows I asked, "What do you mean?"

"Do you ask the blessing before you eat the chips or afterward?" he bantered, enjoying my temporary confusion.

I'm not sure whether it really makes any difference whether we ask God's blessings before or after we eat corn chips or not, but I *am* sure it's important to understand God's timing on the rapture! In fact, understanding the timing is so important that both Paul and Peter prophesied about the dangers of getting it wrong. Paul warned the early church about those who were incorrectly teaching that the rapture had already taken place (as those who hold the preterist doctrine teach today): *"Who concerning the truth have erred, saying that the resurrection is past already; and overthrow the faith of some"* (2 Timothy 2:18 KJV). And Peter prophesied that before the end, some would doubt that Jesus would come back at all!

> *Knowing this first, that there shall come in the last days scoffers, walking after their own lusts, and saying, Where is the promise of his coming? For since the fathers fell asleep, all things continue as they were from the beginning of the creation* (2 Peter 3:3-4 KJV).

TWO DIVERGENT VIEWS

Between these two extremes lies a host of other opinions. In fact, there are probably more divergent views concerning the timing of the rapture than about any other doctrine in Christendom. As my friend alluded to in his jest, two of these stand out above all the rest—pre-tribulation and post-tribulation rapture (usually abbreviated as pre-trib and post-trib).

Those who hold the pre-trib view believe Jesus will return and catch away the Church before the great tribulation that He prophesied in Matthew 24:21. Likewise, those who hold the post-trib view believe the Church will have to endure the tribulation. Lately, the phrase *post-tribulation, pre-wrath rapture* has emerged, which further defines the rapture's timing. This view states that even though the Church will go through the tribulation, believers will be caught up into the air with Jesus before His wrath is poured out upon the earth. Obviously, all these views cannot be right, so which one should we believe?

To answer this question, let's start from the beginning. Paul introduces the doctrine of the rapture in a passage of scripture that is probably read at more funerals than any other scripture in the Bible:

> *But I do not want you to be ignorant, brethren, concerning those who have fallen asleep, lest you sorrow as others who have no hope. For if we believe that Jesus died and rose again, even so God will bring with Him those who sleep in Jesus. For this we say to you by the word of the Lord, that we who are alive and remain **until the coming of the Lord** will by no means precede those who are asleep. For the Lord Himself will descend from heaven with a shout, with the voice of an archangel, and **with the trumpet of God**. And the dead in Christ will rise first. Then we who are alive and remain **shall be caught up** together with them in the clouds to meet the Lord in the air. And thus we shall always be with the Lord. Therefore comfort one another with these words* (1 Thessalonians 4:13-18).

The term *caught up* in verse 17 in this passage is where our English word *rapture* comes from. The words *caught up* are translated from the Greek word *harpazo*, which means to "seize," "catch away," or "catch up."[1] *Harpazo* was translated *raptus* in the Latin translations of the Scriptures and eventually found its way into the English language by being transliterated into the word we use today—*rapture*.

As for the rapture's timing, Paul elaborates on this further in First Corinthians 15:50-52 (KJV):

Now this I say, brethren, that flesh and blood cannot inherit the kingdom of God; neither doth corruption inherit incorruption. Behold, I shew you a mystery; we shall not all sleep, but we shall all be changed, in a moment, in the twinkling of an eye, **at the last trump: for the trumpet shall sound**, *and the dead shall be raised incorruptible, and we shall be changed.*

So from Paul's writing we see that Christ's return will be announced by a trumpet—and not just any trumpet, but by the sounding of the *last* trumpet! This scriptural passage holds the key to determining the rapture's precise timing.

In Matthew 24, after describing the conditions existing before and during the great tribulation, Jesus said:

Immediately after the tribulation of those days *shall the sun be darkened, and the moon shall not give her light, and the stars shall fall from heaven, and the powers of the heavens shall be shaken: and then shall appear the sign of the Son of man in heaven: and then shall all the tribes of the earth mourn, and they shall see the Son of man coming in the clouds of heaven with power and great glory.* **And he shall send his angels with a great sound of a trumpet, and they shall gather together his elect from the four winds, from one end of heaven to the other** (Matthew 24:29-31 KJV).

Although some believe this scripture is referring to Jesus gathering the Jews together and returning them to their land, the presence of the trumpet shows otherwise. If this is not the rapture, then where did the trumpet blast come from?

As we've already seen, Paul said the rapture will occur *"at the last trump."* And here Jesus describes an event that will occur *"immediately after the tribulation"*—which perfectly fits the resurrection—and is accompanied by the *"sound of a trumpet."* The trumpet clearly identifies this gathering together of the elect as the rapture.

The most common objection to this interpretation is twofold. We'll discuss these two points one at a time. We've already mentioned the first objection, which contends, "When Jesus described those who were being gathered, He was talking about the Jews instead of the Church because He used the word *elect* to describe them." The problem with this is the Bible uses *elect* to describe both Jews *and* the Church.

Paul asked, *"Who shall bring a charge against God's elect? It is God who justifies"* (Romans 8:33; see also Colossians 3:12). Likewise, when Peter wrote to the dispersed Christians in Asia, he said they were *"elect according to the foreknowledge of God the Father, in sanctification of the Spirit, for obedience and sprinkling of the blood of Jesus Christ…"* (1 Peter 1:2). And in Second John 1:1, John called the Church "the elect lady." So we see there is no scriptural justification for interpreting Matthew 24:29-31 as a gathering of the Jews, but there is justification for interpreting it as the rapture because of the trumpet that accompanies it.

The second objection to interpreting this event as the rapture claims Jesus was not referring to the rapture when He said, *"…all the tribes of the earth…will see the Son of man coming on the clouds of heaven with power and great glory"* (Matthew 24:30). Those who hold this view argue, "Jesus could not have been talking about the rapture in this verse because the rapture will be secret." But is this correct? Actually, there is not one verse in the Bible that supports a secret rapture! Paul said the rapture will be accompanied by a trumpet. Announcing an event with the blast of a trumpet is probably not the best way to keep it a secret!

When the disciples saw Jesus ascend into the clouds of heaven, the angels who stood by asked them:

> *Men of Galilee, why do you stand gazing up into heaven? This same Jesus, who was taken up from you into heaven, will so come **in like manner** as you saw Him go into heaven* (Acts 1:11).

He didn't leave secretly, and His return is to be "in like manner." John described it the same way Jesus did:

> *Behold, He is coming with clouds, **and every eye will see Him**, even they who pierced Him. And all the tribes of the earth will mourn because of Him. Even so, Amen* (Revelation 1:7).

Everyone will be aware of the rapture when it occurs, and with good reason! You are either going to be in it or suffer the immediate consequences of being left behind. In spite of what some have taught, *there is no second chance.* If you miss the first flight out, you will have to wait a thousand years for the next one—and it's going the wrong way! Immediately after Christ catches up the Church, He is going to commence pouring fire out upon the earth. Paul consoled the persecuted Thessalonians with the promise of God's retribution upon those who were afflicting them. God's fiery retribution will coincide with Christ's return:

And to give you who are troubled rest with us when the Lord Jesus is revealed from heaven with His mighty angels, in flaming fire taking vengeance on those who do not know God, and on those who do not obey the gospel of our Lord Jesus Christ (2 Thessalonians 1:7-8).

THE MARK OF THE BEAST

Regardless of their divergent views on the rapture's actual timing, there are several points in which most theologians are in agreement. One is that the end times will be marked by a seven-year period of time when the antichrist will make a covenant with the Jewish people. After three and a half years, he will break the covenant, and it will be during the latter half of this covenant that the great tribulation will take place. Also, it is generally conceded the mark of the beast will occur sometime during this seven-year period. Jesus said the rapture will take place *"immediately after the tribulation"* (Matthew 24:29), so it is evident that some of those who are caught up in the rapture will have had to endure persecution and will have refused to take the mark of the beast. To this John agrees:

And I saw thrones, and they sat upon them, and judgment was given unto them: and I saw the souls of them that were beheaded for the witness of Jesus, and for the word of God, **and which had not worshiped the beast, neither his image, neither had received his mark** *upon their foreheads, or in their hands; and they lived and reigned with Christ a thousand years. But the rest of the dead lived not again until the thousand years* *were finished. **This is the first resurrection*** (Revelation 20:4-5 KJV).

There can be no doubt. Some of those who are in the rapture, which John calls the "first resurrection," will have been confronted by the antichrist: *"And they overcame him by the blood of the Lamb, and by the word of their testimony; and they loved not their lives unto the death"* (Revelation 12:11 KJV). The rapture is definitely the first resurrection (the second resurrection won't take place until a thousand years later). At the risk of being redundant, I declare once again: there can be no resurrection before the first resurrection, and the first resurrection will include those who have stood faithful unto death during the antichrist's reign! Jesus said the Scripture cannot be broken. It is impossible for the rapture to occur before the antichrist is revealed for who he is. Paul said, *"Let no one deceive you by any means; for that Day will not come unless the falling away comes first, and the man of sin is revealed, the son of perdition"* (2 Thessalonians 2:3).

PERSECUTION

In spite of all the confusion concerning this doctrine, three things are crystal clear: First, the rapture will take place at the blowing of the *last* trumpet. Second, this trumpet won't blow until the tribulation is over. And third, some of those who will be caught up into heaven by the rapture will have been killed because they refused to take the mark of the beast. There is only one inescapable conclusion that fits these three facts—the Church is on a collision course with persecution. Regardless of what one may have been taught, it is certain that the saints *will* go through the tribulation, during which time they *will* be confronted by the mark of the beast.

Since the Scriptures are so plain and clear about the rapture's timing, where did so many different doctrines originate from in the first place? The answer is simple—*fear!* People are deathly afraid of persecution, so anyone who promises them peace and safety is heard and believed. Paul spoke of this in Second Timothy 4:3-4:

> For the time will come when they will not endure sound doctrine, but according to their own desires, because they have itching ears, they will heap up for themselves teachers; and they will turn their ears away from the truth, and be turned aside to fables.

The Bible says that because the end-time, Laodicean church refuses to receive the love of the truth, God will send them a strong delusion, which they will embrace. Because they believe it, they will perish (*Laodicean* means "the people of judgment"[2]). Paul said the antichrist is coming:

> With all unrighteous deception among those who perish, because they did not receive the love of the truth, that they might be saved. And for this reason God will send them strong delusion, that they should **believe the lie**, that they all may be condemned who did not believe the truth but had pleasure in unrighteousness (2 Thessalonians 2:10-12).

THE LIE

And what is *"the lie"* that Paul prophesied of? Jesus is *"the way, **the truth**, and the life"* (John 14:6). Conversely, the antichrist is the (false) way, *the lie,* and the death! The antichrist will tell the world, with convincing proof, that Jesus was a fraud and that *he* is the Messiah. (*Antichrist* is a compound word in Greek. The prefix translated *anti* means "opposite" or "instead of"—so the antichrist is Christ's opposite, taking His place as the savior of the world.[3])

The implications of this lie are enormous. If it were true, it would mean the whole New Testament is false and Jesus is still in the grave. It would mean the Romans were telling the truth when they said Christ's disciples came and stole Him away in the night and buried Him somewhere else (see Matthew 28:13-15). In other words, instead of the Romans, it would mean the apostles conspired to deceive the world—and succeeded!

How is the antichrist going to pull this off? He will use potent, supernatural proof: *"The coming of the lawless one is according to the working of Satan, with all power, signs, and lying wonders"* (2 Thessalonians 2:9). Jesus warned everyone to beware. This deceiver is going to be so convincing that some of the saints will be deceived, and for a season, so will the great majority of the Jews (see Mark 13:22; John 5:43).

OPPOSING VIEWPOINTS

Now we will examine some of the *scriptural* reasons commonly given for opposing the post-tribulation position that we've taken. The first is a statement by Paul found in First Thessalonians 5:9:

For God hath not appointed us to wrath, but to obtain salvation by our Lord Jesus Christ (KJV).

Most people believe the great tribulation with its accompanying persecution is the wrath of God, and because Paul said, *"Jesus...delivered us from the wrath to come,"* they believe it should be obvious that we will not suffer the tribulation (see 1 Thessalonians 1:10 KJV). The problem with this interpretation is the great tribulation isn't *God's* wrath; it's the wrath of *Satan!* God doesn't persecute the saints—Satan does! John reveals the source of Satan's wrath in chapter 12 of Revelation. The devil knows he is running out of time, and he's aware that hell awaits his arrival.

Therefore rejoice, O heavens, and you who dwell in them! Woe to the inhabitants of the earth and the sea! **For the devil** *has come down to you,* **having great wrath, because he knows that he has a short time** (Revelation 12:12).

But didn't Jesus promise the faithful He would spare them from having to go through the great tribulation? To answer that question, let's take a look at what He said and how the rest of Scripture interprets His remarks:

And take heed to yourselves, lest at any time your hearts be overcharged with surfeiting, and drunkenness, and cares of this life, and so that day come upon you unawares. For as a snare shall it come **on all them that dwell on the face of the whole earth.** *Watch ye therefore, and pray always,* **that ye may be accounted worthy to escape all these things that** *shall come to pass*, and to stand before the Son of man (Luke 21:34-36 KJV).

First, there are those who teach that the great tribulation will only be directed toward the Jews, with the express purpose of bringing them back to Christ. Jesus taught otherwise. He warned this end-time sorrow and deception was coming *"on all them that dwell on the face of the whole earth"*—Jews and Gentiles alike. Second, Paul shows us that God's definition of *escape* and our definition are not the same:

> *No temptation has overtaken you except such as is common to man; but God is faithful, who will not allow you to be tempted beyond what you are able, **but with the temptation will also make the way of escape, that you may be able to bear it*** (1 Corinthians 10:13).

God's grace doesn't include deliverance *from* temptation, but rather deliverance from being overcome by the *power* of temptation! In fact, Jesus said, *"...In the world you will have tribulation; but be of good cheer, I have overcome the world"* (John 16:33).

Another reason given for opposing the post-tribulation, pre-wrath rapture is based upon a man-made doctrine called dispensationalism. In essence, this doctrine teaches that God strictly separates His dealings with the Jews and the Church. In other words, since the gathering of Matthew 24:31 is obviously at the very end, and God has promised to restore the Jews to Himself at the end, then Matthew is talking about Christ gathering the Jews back to Israel instead of resurrecting the saints in the rapture.

The problem with this doctrine is that God doesn't agree with it! Paul said God has made the Jews and Gentiles one in Christ. The Jews can only be restored to God by accepting Jesus as their Messiah. Peter, a Jew, said, *"Nor is there salvation in any other, for there is no other name under heaven given among men by which we must be saved"* (Acts 4:12). And Paul said, *"If* [the Jews] *being cast away is the reconciling of the world, what will their acceptance be but life from the dead?"* (Romans 11:15).

So, is Jesus gathering Jews in Matthew 24:31? Possibly, and if they are Messianic Jews, definitely! Does the possibility that He may be gathering Jews preclude Him from gathering His Church at the same time? Certainly not! Paul said that God's acceptance of the Jews *is* the rapture!

The tribulation, with its accompanying persecution (which has rightly been called the time of "Jacob's trouble"), will last about three and one-half years. It will accomplish two things simultaneously. It will purify the Church and at the same time serve to bring the Jews to their knees before their elder brother, Jesus. Scripture puts these two events together for us in chapters 11 and 12 of Daniel. First, the purification and perfection of the Church:

> *And those of the people who understand* [i.e., Christians] *shall instruct many; yet for many days they shall fall by sword and flame, by captivity and plundering. Now when they fall, they shall be aided with a little help; but many shall join with them by intrigue. And some of those of understanding shall fall, to refine them, purify them, and make them white, until the time of the end; because it is still for the appointed time. Then*

the king shall do according to his own will: he shall exalt and magnify himself above every god, shall speak blasphemies against the God of gods, and shall prosper till the wrath has been accomplished; for what has been determined shall be done (Daniel 11:33-36).

To this John agrees, and he also gives us the duration of the antichrist's reign:

So they worshiped the dragon who gave authority to the beast; and they worshiped the beast, saying, "Who is like the beast? Who is able to make war with him?" And he was given a mouth speaking great things and blasphemies, and he was given authority to continue for forty-two months. Then he opened his mouth in blasphemy against God, to blaspheme His name, His tabernacle, and those who dwell in heaven. It was granted to him to make war with the saints and to overcome them. And authority was given him over every tribe, tongue, and nation [Jews and Gentiles] (Revelation 13:4-7).

After describing the effects the end-time persecution will have upon the Church, which John echoes in Revelation, Daniel then turns his focus upon his own people, the Jews:

At that time Michael shall stand up, the great prince who stands watch over the sons of your people; and there shall be a time of trouble, such as never was since there was a nation, even to that time. And at that time your people shall be delivered, every one who is found written in the book. And many of those who sleep in the dust of the earth shall awake, some to everlasting life, some to shame and everlasting contempt. Those who are wise shall shine like the brightness of the firmament, and those who turn many to righteousness like the stars forever and ever (Daniel 12:1-3).

QUESTIONS AND ANSWERS

1. Where does the "secret rapture" doctrine come from? Are there any scriptures to back it up?

This doctrine has taken root because several times Jesus said He was *"coming as a thief"* (see Revelation 3:3; 16:15). Because one characteristic of thieves is they operate in secret, it is assumed that Jesus was saying that His return will be in secret. The problem with this belief is Jesus wasn't talking about coming secretly, but rather coming *unexpectedly*. This is clearly seen in the following scripture:

> *But know this, that if the master of the house had known what hour the thief would come, he would have watched and not allowed his house to be broken into. Therefore you also be ready, for the Son of Man is coming at an hour you do not expect* (Matthew 24:43-44).

2. What is a preterist?

This name is derived from the word *preterit*, which can be defined as that which expresses or describes a past action or condition. Therefore a preterist is one who believes the rapture is past. The most commonly held view is that Jesus came back in A.D. 70 at the time when Jerusalem was destroyed.

The problem is there are no historical records to support this belief, and it would be impossible for an event of such magnitude to occur without being noticed by the public. Also, preterism ignores several events that the Scriptures show must happen before Jesus returns (see the following question).

3. Are there certain events that must occur or conditions that must be met before Christ returns?

There are several specific things that must take place before the rapture occurs. For instance, Jesus said, *"This gospel of the kingdom will be preached in all the world as a witness to all the nations, and then the end will come"* (Matthew 24:14). At present there are about 800 different language groups in the world for which there are no biblical translations. These people have not been sufficiently reached with the gospel message to warrant God bringing them into judgment (see Deuteronomy 17:6). Although this is only one "sign" among many, it is one of the most important.

In Acts 3:20-21, Peter added another dimension to an already complex subject. He said God would:

...send Jesus Christ, who was preached to you before, whom heaven must receive until the times of restoration of all things, which God has spoken by the mouth of all His holy prophets since the world began.

There are still many unfulfilled promises, so the fulfillment of this prophecy may take awhile. Two end-time prophecies of particular interest are Isaiah 30:26 and Acts 2:19-20.

Another condition for the rapture to take place is Christ's Bride has to first "make herself ready" (see Revelation 19:7). Paul said at Christ's return He would *"...present her to Himself a glorious church, not having spot or wrinkle or any such thing, but that she should be holy and without blemish"* (Ephesians 5:27). Obviously, she has some washing and ironing to do, so this may take awhile too!

And last, but not least, Paul gave us a specific warning in Second Thessalonians 2:3:

> *Let no one deceive you by any means; for that Day [of the Lord's return] will not come unless the falling away comes first, and the man of sin is revealed, the son of perdition.*

So Christians can and should expect the antichrist to appear before Jesus returns.

4. What is the exact date of Jesus's return?

Jesus said that no one knows the day or the hour when He will return (see Matthew 25:13). Although we cannot know the precise day and hour, Paul said that we could, and should, know the times and seasons relative to Christ's return (see 1 Thessalonians 5:1-6).

5. Some people teach that instead of the righteous being taken out, Jesus is going to take the wicked out of the earth and leave the Church. What is the scriptural basis for this doctrine?

This belief is primarily based on the parable of the tares found in Matthew 13:24-30, in which the wheat represents the righteous and the tares represent the wicked. Jesus said:

Let both [the tares and the wheat] *grow together until the harvest, and at the time of harvest I will say to the reapers, "First gather together the tares and bind them in bundles to burn them, but gather the wheat into my barn"* (Matthew 13:30).

The error here is this parable is actually about the wicked who are presently in the church, not those who are in the world. Jesus declared:

I am the vine, ye are the branches: He that abides in me, and I in him, the same brings forth much fruit.... If a man abide not in me, he is cast forth as a branch, and is withered; and men gather them, and cast them into the fire, and they are burned (John 15:5-6 KJV).

Peter said:

For the time is come that judgment must begin at the house of God: and if it first begin at us, what shall the end be of them that obey not the gospel of God? And if the righteous scarcely be saved, where shall the ungodly and the sinner appear? (1 Peter 4:17-18 KJV)

Before the rapture and the ensuing fiery destruction, God is going to cleanse the temple once more (see John 2:13-16; Matthew 21:12). For the Bride to be without spot or wrinkle, the tares—such as hirelings, hypocrites, etc.—have to be removed (see John 10:12-13; Matthew 15:7-9).

6. Is the rapture mentioned in the Book of Revelation?

Yes, more than once. The Book of Revelation is composed of four visions. The rapture is alluded to in three of them (see Revelation 7:9-17; 14:14-16; 20:4-6). For example, both of the earth's end-time harvests are described in chapter 14 of Revelation. The first is the post-tribulation, pre-wrath rapture, which takes place after the sounding of the seventh and last trumpet (see Revelation 10:7; 11:15). The second harvest is the fiery indignation of the wrath of God:

> *Then I looked, and behold, a white cloud, and on the cloud sat One like the Son of Man, having on His head a golden crown, and in His hand a sharp sickle. And another angel came out of the temple, crying with a loud voice to Him who sat on the cloud, "Thrust in Your sickle and reap, for the time has come for You to reap, for the harvest of the earth is ripe." So He who sat on the cloud thrust in His sickle on the earth, and the earth was reaped.*

> *Then another angel came out of the temple which is in heaven, he also having a sharp sickle. And another angel came out from the altar, who had power over fire, and he cried with a loud cry to him who had the sharp sickle, saying, "Thrust in your sharp sickle and gather the clusters of the vine of the earth, for her grapes are fully ripe." So the angel thrust his sickle into the earth and gathered the vine of the earth, and threw it into the great winepress of the wrath of God* (Revelation 14:14-19).

7. What does the Bible mean when it refers to a trumpet sounding?

A trumpet sounding is the revelation and proclamation of an existing condition or an approaching event. Its revelation is usually revealed through preaching. For example, Isaiah 58:1 says, *"Cry aloud, spare not; lift up your voice like a trumpet; tell My people their transgression, and the house of Jacob their sins."* Another example is John the Baptist's introduction of Jesus as the Messiah. God always precedes His work with His Word (see Amos 3:7). He speaks and whatever He says comes to pass. For example, the first six trumpets of Revelation declare—and therefore release onto the earth—the horrible conditions of the great tribulation. The seventh declares and releases both the rapture and the wrath of God (God's wrath is contained in the seven vials, or bowls, which follow).

8. Some theologians teach the last trumpet that Paul prophesied of in First Corinthians 15:52 refers to the Jewish Feast of Trumpets, and is not to be confused with the trumpets of Revelation. Is this true?

There is absolutely no biblical support for that position. Both Paul's "last trumpet" and John's seventh (and last) trumpet announce the first resurrection. John didn't prophesy in a vacuum. Scripture always interprets Scripture. At the sounding of Revelation's seventh and last trumpet, John wrote:

But in the days of the sounding of the seventh angel, when he is about to sound, the mystery of God would be finished, as He declared to His servants the prophets (Revelation 10:7).

Then the seventh angel sounded: and there were loud voices in heaven, saying, "The kingdoms of this world

*have become the kingdoms of our Lord and of His
Christ, and He shall reign forever and ever!"* (Revelation 11:15)

It cannot get any plainer than that! The seventh trumpet
announces Christ's final conquest of the kingdoms of this
world. And as we saw above, it initiates the first resurrection
(rapture) and sets the stage for the beginning of the outpouring of God's wrath upon the earth.

9. What is the significance of the antichrist's number, 666? Is it literal or symbolic?

To answer this question, we first need to examine the
passage in Revelation where John talks about 666:

> *And I beheld another beast coming up out of the earth;
> and he had two horns like a lamb, and he spake as a
> dragon.*
>
> *Here is wisdom. Let him that hath understanding
> count the number of the beast: for it is the number of a
> man; and his number is Six hundred threescore and six*
> (Revelation 13:11,18 KJV).

The whole of Revelation is symbolic, so we can safely
assume that this number is symbolic as well. John identifies
the beast as a man. Since we know that this is an evil man,
we also know the symbolism used here is negative. Thus, the
interpretation is simply this: six portrays an *image*, which
John plainly declared is the image of man; sixty means a
rejected image; and six hundred describes a *full* image. So,
in the same way that Christ was the express image of the
invisible God, this beastly man will be the warped image of

the invisible devil. He will be Christ's exact opposite. He will *fully* reflect Satan's *despicable image*.

RECOMMENDED READING

Understanding the Dreams You Dream, Volume II by Ira L. Milligan (formerly titled *Every Dreamer's Handbook*). Christians have been mystified for years by the number 666 attributed to the beast in Revelation 13:18 and the *"one hundred and forty-four thousand"* sealed in Revelation 7:4. As the answer to question 9 above reveals, understanding Revelation's symbolism requires an understanding of biblical numerology, which is provided in this book. Chapter Three gives a more complete understanding of the symbolism of the number 666.

ENDNOTE

1. *Strong's Exhaustive Concordance* (Thomas Nelson, 1990), Greek #726.

2. *Strong's*, Greek #2994, from 2992 and 1349.

3. *Strong's*, Greek #500, from 473 and 5547.

> *Therefore whoever confesses Me before men, him I will also confess before My Father who is in heaven* (**Matthew 10:32**).

Chapter Three

POSITIVE CONFESSION

The following is a portion of one of the saddest letters that I have ever received. After reading it, my heart ached for this family. I think yours will too, unless you are laboring under the same delusion the pastor referred to in this letter is under. (I've changed the names, places, and dates to protect the innocent).

Dear Mr. Milligan,

I am writing to ask you to pray for my husband. We lost a big construction company in Tennessee in 2004. My husband has come close to having a nervous breakdown. We are tithers and givers. We are givers with joy! The church that we attend does not believe in personal ministry. Neither do they believe in counseling. They believe that if you attend church and read or own a Bible, that is all you need. Well, I disagree.

What we are going through is too big for my husband's faith. He needs others to lift him up. We attended a church (a Rhema church) where faith is strongly taught. The minister is an AWESOME teacher but no one has reached out to my husband. Our pastor was told what we were going through in detail. He did call to see if my husband was making his confessions. When he said, "Not always," the pastor said, "Just one time of not making your confessions can void out all the rest," which I disagree with. I do believe that we need to make confessions of the Word (God's promises).

My husband is talking about death. He is a born-again, Spirit-filled Christian, but he said he feels like giving up. Would you pray for him?

An "AWESOME" teacher of what? God's Word or man's deception? Jesus said, *"…The truth shall make you free"* (John 8:32). Conversely, error and deception will enslave you, and, as we can see from the letter above, possibly even destroy you! This letter is a good example of the severe consequences of false doctrine. But where does such error originate from?

A wise Christian historian observed that every major heresy in Christianity started with a minor deviation from the truth. The "positive confession" (or as its critics call it, "name it and claim it") doctrine is no exception. The road to heaven is littered with the souls of those wounded and destroyed by "pastors" teaching doctrines like the one illustrated above. Telling someone in trouble, "All you need is the Bible" is tantamount to saying, "I don't have answers to your questions, solutions for your problems, or time to waste upon you." It's an excuse, not a solution.

In my opinion, a shepherd who doesn't believe in personal ministry or counseling shouldn't be allowed into the pulpit. Such a person is a disgrace to his or her profession. God expects His shepherds to tend His flocks, not just fleece them at shearing time. He also expects them to study and meditate upon His Word so that when they do minister to His sheep, their words will bring healing and wholeness, not despair and hopelessness (see Malachi 2:7; 2 Timothy 2:15).

THE LIVING WORD

God and His Word are one, *but the Bible isn't God!* The Bible is the record of God's dealings with humankind, showing us His ways, which never change, and His works, which are forever changing. The way He dealt with Abraham thousands of years ago is the same way He still deals with us today. Our righteousness is by faith, but that faith should be based upon His whole *living* Word, not just one select portion of the Logos. Jesus said, *"...Man shall not live by bread alone, but by **every word** [rhema in Greek] that proceeds from the mouth of God"* (Matthew 4:4). It takes fresh whole wheat to make fresh, wholesome bread!

As Paul said, we need to examine closely *"what saith the scripture?"* (see Romans 4:3 KJV) concerning the modern confession doctrine if we want to separate the wheat from the chaff. It originated in the mid-nineteenth century and was popularized in the latter half of the twentieth century. This basic doctrine can be summed up in the statement: "You must confess it to possess it." Is this true? And whether true or not, where did it come from?

One of the primary scriptures used to support this doctrine is Romans 10:8-10:

> *But what does it* [the righteousness of faith] *say? "The word is near you, in your mouth and in your heart" (that is, the word of faith which we preach): that if you confess with your mouth the Lord Jesus and believe in your heart that God has raised Him from the dead, you will be saved. For with the heart one believes unto righteousness, and with the mouth confession is made unto salvation.*

Although the confession doctrine's platform stops here, Paul didn't. He went on to say:

> *For there is no distinction between Jew and Greek, for the same Lord over all is rich to all who call upon Him. For "whoever calls on the name of the Lord shall be saved." How then shall they call on Him in whom they have not believed? And how shall they believe in Him of whom they have not heard? And how shall they hear without a preacher?* (Romans 10:12-14)

The key words are, *"How shall they hear without a preacher?"* When preachers seek God, listen to what He tells them to tell His people, and faithfully deliver His message, they bless and benefit the people. But just preaching something because it is in the written Word is doing nothing more than the scribes of Jesus's day were doing. *"The letter kills, but the Spirit gives life"* (2 Corinthians 3:6). The Word without the Spirit is death. Only the inspired, living word that proceeds forth from the mouth of God gives life.

Faith comes by hearing. It is the product of hearing what God is presently saying—not reading, memorizing, and repeating what He has said in the past. God never intended for His people to try to use His Word without seeking Him to know His will. The Bible doesn't give us formulas; it gives us knowledge of how to enter into God's presence and receive *"grace to help in time of need"* (Hebrews 4:16). A perfect example is Psalm 91:10-12 (KJV):

> *There shall no evil befall thee, neither shall any plague come nigh thy dwelling. For he shall give his angels charge over thee, to keep thee in all thy ways. They shall bear thee up in their hands, lest thou dash thy foot against a stone.*

When Satan tempted Christ and challenged Him to prove that He was the Son of God, this is one of the scriptures he quoted. Jesus responded, *"It is said, Thou shalt not tempt the Lord thy God"* (Luke 4:12). Even the promise of angels guarding the Son of God was conditional. And it was not only conditional, it was totally ineffective until put into operation—not through confession, but by prayer based upon it!

When Jesus was being arrested in the Garden of Gethsemane, Peter attempted to defend Him, but Jesus told him:

> *Put your sword in its place, for all who take the sword will perish by the sword. Or do you think that I cannot now pray to My Father, and He will provide Me with more than twelve legions of angels?* (Matthew 26:52-53)

In spite of the fact that God had given a specific promise for His protection, it was necessary for Jesus to pray before that protection came into play (and when He didn't ask, it wasn't provided). Doesn't it stand to reason that if the Son of God had to pray to receive the promises, we have to do the same? As we can see, Paul's concept of salvation through confessing Christ and the concept of verbally confessing the promises to initiate their fulfillment aren't exactly the same thing.

THE NEED TO ASK

Also, we should ask, does this scripture stand alone, or are there other conditions that must be met besides confession and prayer before the desired results are achieved? The Bible gives several, but one stands out above all the rest—our requests must be according to the will of God. John said:

> *Now this is the confidence that we have in Him, that if we ask anything according to His will, He hears us. And if we know that He hears us, whatever we ask, we know that we have the petitions that we have asked of Him* (1 John 5:14-15).

An excellent example of praying to know the will of God is David in the valley of Rephaim:

> *The Philistines also went and deployed themselves in the Valley of Rephaim. So David inquired of the Lord, saying, "Shall I go up against the Philistines? Will You deliver them into my hand?"* **And the Lord said to**

*David, **"Go up**, for I will doubtless deliver the Philis-*
tines into your hand." So David went to Baal Perazim,
and David defeated them there....

Then the Philistines went up once again and deployed
*themselves in the Valley of Rephaim. Therefore **David***
inquired of the Lord, and He said, "You shall not
***go up**; circle around behind them, and come upon them*
in front of the mulberry trees. And it shall be, when you
hear the sound of marching in the tops of the mulberry
trees, then you shall advance quickly. For then the Lord
will go out before you to strike the camp of the Phi-
listines." And David did so, as the Lord commanded
him; and he drove back the Philistines... (2 Samuel
5:18-20;22-25).

David, who was under divine orders to shepherd God's
people and deliver them from their enemies, wisely inquired
before going into battle. The first time God said, "Go up."
The second time He said, "You shall not go up." Even though
the second threat was identical to the first, God's strategy,
including His timing, was different. Therefore His will had
changed accordingly.

A minister who practiced the positive confession doctrine
and wrote a book on it later realized that he was wrong. He
confessed and admitted that his group had reached a point
where they actually thought it was a sin to pray—because if
they had to ask, they were not operating in faith! Thankfully,
God mercifully sent him a prophet and showed him the error
of his ways (and doctrine).

Faith comes by hearing, and hearing comes in many different ways. It may come through prayer, meditating upon God's Word, interpreting our dreams, or listening to His anointed messengers who themselves have spent time in His presence listening to Him. Sometimes God even speaks through the circumstances of our lives. His will always conforms to His Word, but His Word is quite complex and covers every side of every situation. There's no way around it—we have to ask, and He has to point out what promises apply in our present time of need before we can obtain what we are seeking.

God said:

"Incline your ear, and come to Me. Hear, and your soul shall live; and I will make an everlasting covenant with you—the sure mercies of David."

Seek the Lord while He may be found, call upon Him while He is near.

"For My thoughts are not your thoughts, nor are your ways My ways," says the Lord. "For as the heavens are higher than the earth, so are My ways higher than your ways, and My thoughts than your thoughts" (Isaiah 55:3,6,8-9).

We are not only ignorant of God's ways without asking, we don't even know our *own* ways without asking! Proverbs 20:24 says, *"A man's steps are of the Lord; how then can a man understand his own way?"* Paul said, *"Therefore do not be unwise, but understand what the will of the Lord is"* (Ephesians 5:17). How can we understand without asking?

THE HEARING OF FAITH

Another popular scripture used when teaching the positive confession doctrine is Mark 11:22-23:

So Jesus answered and said to them, "Have faith in God. For assuredly, I say to you, whoever says to this mountain, 'Be removed and be cast into the sea,' and does not doubt in his heart, but believes that those things he says will be done, he will have whatever he says."

Again, this is a conditional promise. The condition? That whoever is praying *"does not doubt in his heart, but believes that those things he says will be done."* And where does such faith come from? Read Jesus's preface to the promise again— *"Have faith in God."* Whether saving faith or faith to move the mountain, it's all the same. Faith comes—and only comes—by hearing God. Paul said, *"For by grace you have been saved through faith, and that* [faith is] *not of yourselves; **it is the gift of God"*** (Ephesians 2:8).

Faith comes from hearing and believing the rhema word God is presently speaking. If one hasn't received a specific rhema from God to move the mountain, it will still be there a thousand years after being commanded to leave. The heart has to be convinced by hearing God, otherwise it will remain in doubt regardless of how many times one confesses the promises.

Why then did Jesus tell us to speak to the mountain when we need it to move? Why didn't He tell us to ask Him to move it instead? The answer is found by examining another similar passage of scripture, in which Jesus reveals the source of His authority to command miracles into existence:

And seeing a fig tree by the road, He came to it and found nothing on it but leaves, and said to it, "Let no fruit grow on you ever again." Immediately the fig tree withered away.

*And when the disciples saw it, they marveled, saying, "How did the fig tree wither away so soon?" So Jesus answered and said to them, "Assuredly, I say to you, if you have faith and do not doubt, you will not only do what was done to the fig tree, but also if you say to this mountain, 'Be removed and be cast into the sea,' it will be done. And whatever things you **ask in prayer**, believing, you will receive"* (Matthew 21:19-22).

The last part of this passage reveals that Jesus had already petitioned the Father about His will concerning the tree before He cursed it. The procedure is simple. We first petition God for what we need—as in the case of the mountain, we ask Him to remove it—and then we wait for His answer. If He rejects our request, the mountain stays put. If He accepts our petition and answers in the affirmative, His acceptance gives us the authority to speak to it in His name, which releases the power to move it out of our way. Paul tells us that receiving from God and ministering for God are both accomplished the same way. Not by the *confession* of faith, but by *"the **hearing** of faith"*:

*This only I want to learn from you: Did you receive the Spirit by the works of the law, or by **the hearing of faith**?*

*Therefore He who **supplies** the Spirit to you and **works miracles** among you, does He do it by the works of the law, or by **the hearing of faith**?* (Galatians 3:2,5)

Jesus said, *"Ask, and it will be given to you,"* not "Confess and you shall receive" (see Luke 11:9).

What purpose does the written Word serve then, if we always have to go to God anyway? What value is it? The Word's value is immeasurable. Without it we wouldn't even know that we can go to Him in our time of need. We wouldn't know anything about Him. We wouldn't know Who He is, what His nature is, or how He deals with humankind. We wouldn't know about the covenant that He has made with us through His Son or its many benefits—in fact, without His Word we wouldn't even know who His Son is! In other words, God's Word teaches us everything we need to know about Him and His purposes so that we can believe Him when He does speak to us. Likewise, His Word reveals who our archenemy is so that we can wisely separate God's voice from his.

God's Word is invaluable, but it is not a book of formulas to memorize and use as magic potions to get what we want. God and His Word are one. But God is a living, thinking, loving being—not a machine to activate by quoting the right scripture or confessing the right promise at just the right time.

QUESTIONS AND ANSWERS

1. Doesn't the Bible say that death and life are in the power of the tongue?

Yes (see Proverbs 18:21), but like all Scripture, this proverb has to be taken in light of many others. For instance, if a man dies, telling him that he isn't dead doesn't change his condition. Jesus said, *"It is the Spirit who gives life; the flesh profits nothing. The words that I speak to you are spirit, and they are life"* (John 6:63). Even receiving salvation through confessing Christ as our Lord and Savior requires divine assistance and intervention. Paul said, *"For by grace you have been saved through faith, **and that not of yourselves**; it is the gift of God"* (Ephesians 2:8). And, *"…no one can say that Jesus is Lord except by the Holy Spirit"* (1 Corinthians 12:3).

2. If the Bible makes a promise, doesn't that automatically give us the authority to believe it and act upon it?

No, it gives us the privilege of asking for its fulfillment. It is up to God to determine whether or not to give us what we are asking for. For example, even if the Bible promises something, if we ask for it with the wrong motives we usually won't receive it. James said, *"…you do not have because you do not ask. You ask and do not receive, because you ask amiss, that you may spend it on your pleasures"* (James 4:2-3).

3. Doesn't the Bible teach us to publicly confess the promises?

No! There are forty-four verses that refer to confession in the Bible and *not one* of them teaches us to confess the promises—publicly or otherwise. The Bible teaches us to publicly confess Jesus as Lord and to privately confess our sins to God or to one another (see Romans 10:9; Matthew 10:32; Psalm

32:5; Proverbs 28:13; 1 John 1:9; James 5:16). There is not a single scripture telling us to *confess* the promises, but there are many teaching us to *pray* the promises. For example, personal rhema promises usually require acceptance and then a prayer of agreement before they will come to pass.

One example is Mary's acceptance of the angel Gabriel's message concerning the conception of Jesus when he announced it to her (see Luke 1:38). Another is when Nathan came to David and told him that God had promised to build him a house (see 2 Samuel 7:11). David immediately began praying for God to fulfill His promise. His prayer is a beautiful model of how we should respond to God's precious promises, including the written ones:

> *For You, O Lord of hosts, God of Israel, have revealed this to Your servant, saying, "I will build you a house." Therefore Your servant has found it in his heart to pray this prayer to You. And now, O Lord God, You are God, and Your words are true, and You have promised this goodness to Your servant. Now therefore, let it please You to bless the house of Your servant, that it may continue before You forever; for You, O Lord God, have spoken it, and with Your blessing let the house of Your servant be blessed forever* (2 Samuel 7:27-29).

4. What about Philemon 1:6? (*"That the sharing of your faith may become effective by the acknowledgment of every good thing which is in you in Christ Jesus."*) Doesn't this scripture say that we must confess the promises?

No, it doesn't! Read it again. It has nothing to do with God's written promises. Paul said that before our faith is effective, we must acknowledge that which God has placed *within us,* not confess that which He promised in His Word. When God speaks a rhema to our hearts or gives us a vision, we cannot act in faith until we acknowledge what we hear or see. For example, Jeremiah had to first acknowledge the vision God gave him before he was told what it meant:

> *Moreover the word of the Lord came to me, saying, "Jeremiah, what do you see?" And I said, "I see a branch of an almond tree." Then the Lord said to me, "You have seen well, for I am ready to perform My word"* (Jeremiah 1:11-12).

A thought unspoken dies unborn. We must acknowledge the thoughts and visions that God puts into our hearts or we will never act upon them.

5. Those who believe the positive confession doctrine teach that we are "little gods," and because we are gods, we have authority to act and speak as gods. Is this correct?

No. Those who quote the scripture that says, "You are gods" and use it to justify their heresy have neglected to read the rest of what it says: *"I said, 'You are gods, and all of you are children of the Most High. But you shall die like men, and fall like one of the princes'"* (Psalm 82:6-7; see also Isaiah 41:21-25).

We are *gods* because we are children of God. But, because we are *children,* we are subject to our Heavenly Father's authority. We are not an authority unto ourselves, authorized to do and say anything we want to say or do.

Chapter Four

FIRE INSURANCE

Several years ago, I counseled a middle-aged, Christian man who was having marital problems. As he confessed the many trysts and extramarital affairs in his past, I said, "It was a good thing that you didn't die while all that was going on or you would have busted hell wide open!" His reply shocked me: "Oh no," he exclaimed, "I had fire insurance." I was incredulous. *"Fire insurance?* Are you telling me that you actually believe that if you had died while living in adultery, that you would have gone to heaven?" "Oh yes," he replied, "My dad was a deacon. I've been saved since I was seven years old."

After pointing out certain scriptures to him, I asked him if he still believed that he would have gone to heaven had he died during that time. He said, "Not according to *those* scriptures!" My reply was to assure him that those scriptures were just as important as the ones that he thought supplied him with fire insurance. We must live by *every* word of God, not just the ones we like to hear and want to believe.

Jesus confronted the Pharisees for this same type of blindness. He scolded them:

You search the Scriptures, for in them you think you have eternal life; and these are they which testify of Me. But you are not willing to come to Me that you may have life (John 5:39-40).

Eternity is too long and hell is too hot to take unnecessary chances.

This man's attitude toward sin reminded me of a scripture in Jeremiah:

Behold, you trust in lying words that cannot profit. Will you steal, murder, commit adultery, swear falsely, burn incense to Baal, and walk after other gods whom you do not know, and then come and stand before Me in this house which is called by My name, and say, "We are delivered to do all these abominations"? (Jeremiah 7:8-10)

God's grace is beyond our comprehension, but regardless of how wonderful grace is, it still doesn't give us license to sin. Paul asked, *"What then? Shall we sin, because we are not under the law, but under grace? **God forbid**"* (Romans 6:15 KJV). What God forbids, no person has the right to authorize! Proverbs 14:12 says, *"There is a way that seems right to a man, but its end is the way of death."* This admonition is so important that Solomon repeated it again in Proverbs 16:25. Beware! What you don't know about the Word of God can *kill* you!

There's only one gospel, so let's find it in Scripture. Paul enumerated it for us in First Corinthians.

*Moreover, brethren, **I declare to you the gospel** which I preached to you, which also you received and in which you stand, **by which also you are saved, if you hold fast that word which I preached to you**— unless you believed in vain. For I delivered to you first of all that which I also received: that Christ died for our sins according to the Scriptures, and that He was buried, and that He rose again the third day according to the Scriptures, and that He was seen by Cephas, then by the twelve.*

Then last of all He was seen by me also, as by one born out of due time (1 Corinthians 15:1-5,8).

As one can see, the gospel is the death, burial, resurrection, and the witness of the resurrection of Jesus Christ. Paul assures us that this gospel saves us *if* we continue in these things. In Romans Paul further teaches us that we "obey" the gospel by dying with Christ in repentance, being buried with Him through baptism, and rising from the grave with Him by walking in righteousness:

Therefore we were buried with Him through baptism into death, that just as Christ was raised from the dead by the glory of the Father, even so we also should walk in newness of life. For if we have been united together in the likeness of His death, certainly we also shall be in the likeness of His resurrection, knowing this, that our old man was crucified with Him, that the body of sin might be done away with, that we should no longer be slaves of sin.

Therefore do not let sin reign in your mortal body, that you should obey it in its lusts. And do not present your members as instruments of unrighteousness to sin, but present yourselves to God as being alive from the dead, and your members as instruments of righteousness to God. For sin shall not have dominion over you, for you are not under law but under grace (Romans 6:4-6;12-14).

Thus Paul, the great apostle of grace, assures us that through the gospel we are delivered from the power of sin; therefore we shouldn't allow it to reign in our mortal bodies anymore. In fact, he *forbids* us from doing so. In other words, his answer to Jeremiah's question quoted above is, "No, we are *not* delivered to do all these abominations."

Where did the idea originate that once we are saved, it really doesn't matter how we live? Although those who teach *eternal security* (the real name of the "once-saved, always-saved" doctrine) don't actually say that it doesn't matter, that is the natural consequence of their doctrine. If Christians are saved and cannot lose their salvation, why should they deny themselves the pleasures of sin?

Before we investigate the scriptural root of this doctrine, let me ask a question: why is it that many Christians believe that salvation is a choice, yet once they are saved they can no longer choose? Initially, we are free to accept or reject Christ as Savior. But once the choice is made to accept Him, according to this doctrine we lose our free will and we cannot go back.

The truth is, like the man who foolishly trusted in a fire insurance policy issued by a fraudulent company from hell, many do change their minds after they are saved and return to sin. When they do, they are lost. John said, *"...Let no one deceive you. He who practices righteousness is righteous.... He who sins is of the devil..."* (1 John 3:7-8). Those who are "of the devil" are certainly not going to dwell eternally in heaven with Christ!

So where does the once-saved, always-saved belief come from? One scripture that is often quoted in support of this doctrine is Hebrews 10:14: *"For by one offering [Christ] has perfected forever those who are being sanctified."* However, people who use this verse to support once-saved, always-saved are taking it out of context. They are ignoring the rest of what the writer says. Only twelve verses later he says, *"For if we sin willfully after we have received the knowledge of the truth, there no longer remains a sacrifice for sins"* (Hebrews 10:26). So, clearly, verse 14's "perfected forever" doesn't mean a person who is perfected cannot turn back and forsake his or her relationship with God.

What does it mean then? It means that once someone has accepted Christ as his Lord and Savior and repented of his sins, those sins will never be remembered and charged to his account again. From that point on, he has eternal life. But if he becomes disobedient and turns away from God, back to sin, he will lose his salvation.

If we walk in the Spirit, in obedience to the gospel, we are saved. If we foolishly yield to Satan's deceptions and sin, we are in trouble with God. If we sin, He will chasten us as children. If we repent, His blood will cleanse us from our unrighteousness and purify our hearts anew. If we harden our hearts and continue in sin, we perish. It's that simple. Paul's *if* in First Corinthians 15:2 cannot be ignored (*"...you are saved, **if** you hold fast that word which I preached to you..."*).

When asked about those who were once saved who die in sin, those who hold the eternal security doctrine simply say they were never saved to begin with. They usually quote John 10:27-28, where Jesus said:

> *My sheep hear My voice, and I know them, and they follow Me. And I give them eternal life, and they shall never perish; neither shall anyone snatch them out of My hand.*

And it is certainly true that no one can take them out of the Savior's hand, but it is also true that if they decide to leave Christ's hand, they are not going to be held against their will! (See Hebrews 11:15.)

Solomon said, *"I saw the wicked buried, who had come and gone from the place of the holy..."* (Ecclesiastes 8:10 KJV). Some Christians leave *"the place of the holy"* and return to the things they loved before they knew Christ. A good New Testament example is Demas. Two of Paul's Epistles include Demas as one of his fellow laborers (see Colossians 4:14; Philemon 1:24). Then Paul wrote, *"Demas has forsaken me, having loved this present world..."* (2 Timothy 4:10). Demas forsook more than Paul; he forsook his salvation too. John said, *"Love not the world, neither the things that are in the world. If any man love the world, the love of the Father is not in him"* (1 John 2:15 KJV).

When Demas allowed Satan to seduce his soul and draw him back into the world, he turned away from God (see Hebrews 10:38). The fact that Demas turned back does not mean that he never started out in the first place. Paul would have never considered someone a fellow laborer unless he or she was saved.

SALVATION

At this point, maybe we should ask: How do we know if someone is really saved? What actually happens to someone when they are truly "born again"? To fully answer these questions, we need to examine something Peter said in First Peter 3:21 (KJV):

> *The like figure whereunto even baptism doth also now save us (not the putting away of the filth of the flesh, but the answer of a good conscience toward God,) by the resurrection of Jesus Christ.*

Peter is quite specific about what saves us—*baptism.* No, not water baptism, but rather the *baptism of faith.* The first thing that happens when we are saved is our hearts respond with *"the answer of a good conscience toward God."* (The *"putting away of the filth of the flesh"* is the baptism of repentance, as in John's baptism—see Acts 19:4—and although repentance is necessary, repentance alone is not enough.) The first work of grace is to purify our conscience from the defilement of sin. The writer of Hebrews asks:

> *For if the blood of bulls and goats…sanctifies for the purifying of the flesh, how much more shall the blood of*

*Christ…**cleanse your conscience** from dead works to serve the living God?* (Hebrews 9:13-14)

Therefore, in its simplest terms, salvation is a matter of obtaining and maintaining a pure, undefiled conscience. That is one of the primary reasons Jesus said that to enter the Kingdom of God one must become as a little child. People are born again when, through faith, they believe from their hearts that God has accepted them in Christ and has forgiven them of their sins.

That's why Paul said that he always strove *"to have a conscience without offense toward God and men"* (Acts 24:16). Paul was saved and he wanted to stay that way! He also admonished Timothy about the dangers of not maintaining a clear conscience: *"Keeping faith and a good conscience, which some have rejected and suffered shipwreck in regard to their faith"* (1 Timothy 1:19 NASB).

It is impossible to have faith and a condemned conscience at the same time. If you reject the voice of your conscience, you endanger your soul. When a Christian ceases listening to his or her conscience and yields to temptation, he sins. James said:

> *Every man is tempted, when he is drawn away of his own lust, and enticed. Then when lust has conceived, it brings forth sin: and sin, when it is finished, brings forth death* (James 1:14-15 KJV).

What is the conclusion? Paul sums it up, *"For if you live according to the flesh you will die; but if by the Spirit you put to death the deeds of the body, you will live"* (Romans 8:13).

Genuine salvation consists of love out of a pure heart, a good conscience, and sincere faith (see 1 Timothy 1:5). Or, as one Old Testament prophet wrote:

> *He has shown you, O man, what is good; and what does the Lord require of you but to do justly, to love mercy, and to walk humbly with your God?* (Micah 6:8)

All else is deception.

PREDESTINATION

Peter said that we are saved by the baptism of faith, and Paul concurred, stating, *"For by grace you have been saved through faith, and that not of yourselves; it is the gift of God"* (Ephesians 2:8). But this verse, and several others that refer to predestination, have been a bone of contention among theologians for centuries. Why? Because Paul said that saving faith was "not of yourselves." Some have read these words and concluded, "If salvation is not of ourselves, then salvation must be a sovereign work of God, and we have nothing to do with it. God has already predestined us to either heaven or hell, and we have no choice in the matter!"

But is that what Paul actually meant when he said that saving faith is not of ourselves but rather is a gift from God? And do the Scriptures actually say that we are predestined to either heaven or hell?

To find the answer to those questions, let's first examine Paul's phrase "not of yourselves." If our eternal destiny is pre-determined, what is the purpose of calling upon the name of the Lord, as Paul instructed us to do in Romans 10:13? *"For whosoever shall call upon the name of the Lord shall be saved"* (KJV). The answer is that when sinners call upon the Lord **in** their lost state, He responds by giving them the gift of faith to be saved. Therefore, Paul could rightly say to them, "Your faith is not of yourselves; it is the gift of God" (see Ephesians 2:8).

It is important to make the distinction between faith and salvation. Paul didn't say that your *salvation* was "not of yourselves" (i.e., not an act of your own will), but rather that your *faith* was "not of yourselves."

As for the doctrine of *predestination* (found only in Paul's writings), its true meaning may surprise you. Before discussing predestination, we should examine the four verses containing this word—two in Romans and two in Ephesians:

> *For whom he did foreknow,* **he also did predestinate to be conformed to the image of his Son**, *that he might be the firstborn among many brethren. Moreover whom he did predestinate, them he also called: and whom he called, them he also justified: and whom he justified, them he also glorified* (Romans 8:29-30 KJV).

> *Having predestinated us unto the adoption of children by Jesus Christ to himself, according to the good pleasure of his will.*

> *In whom also we have obtained an inheritance, being predestinated according to the purpose of him who works all things after the counsel of his own will* (Ephesians 1:5,11 KJV).

Condensing all four verses into one, we have these facts: God has foreknowledge of certain people, whom He calls. He has predestined (predetermined) that all who answer His call must conform to the image of His Son. Those who respond, He adopts, justifies, and glorifies. If we add the sum of what we have previously discussed to this, we have the following: If those who are called and adopted continue with Him in obedience to the gospel, they will abide eternally with Him in heaven. Those who refuse His call, or initially respond but afterward fall away, will be forever lost. Either way, He already knows in advance both *who* and *how many* will respond to His call and be saved.

From this summation arises the legitimate question, does Paul mean that God has predetermined to send certain individuals to hell and receive others into heaven? Or does he simply mean that God knows in advance who will answer His call and allow Him to conform them into the image of His Son? A close examination reveals that the latter is actually what He has predetermined—not whether certain individuals are going to heaven or hell. In other words, if you are going to be an eternal son of His, you are going to think and act like His only begotten Son. Your conduct is not left up to you.

QUESTIONS AND ANSWERS

1. Are there any scriptures that actually say that a person committing adultery will be denied entrance into heaven?

Yes, there are, and not only adultery but many other sins as well:

> *Do you not know that the unrighteous will not inherit the kingdom of God? Do not be deceived. Neither fornicators, nor idolaters, nor adulterers, nor homosexuals, nor sodomites, nor thieves, nor covetous, nor drunkards, nor revilers, nor extortioners will inherit the kingdom of God* (1 Corinthians 6:9-10; see also Galatians 5:19-21; Hebrews 12:14-15).

2. Is inheriting the Kingdom of God mentioned in the above scripture synonymous with being saved and going to heaven?

Yes, when Paul expounded upon the resurrection of the dead that is to take place at the rapture, he referred directly to those who would, and would not, inherit the Kingdom of God. He said:

> *Now this I say, brethren, that flesh and blood cannot inherit the kingdom of God…. Behold, I tell you a mystery: we shall not all sleep, but we shall all be changed* (1 Corinthians 15:50-51; see also Luke 18:24-26).

3. What is the significance that the (supposed) doctrine of predestination only appears in Paul's writing?

Paul assured us that *"…by the mouth of two or three witnesses every word shall be established"* (2 Corinthians 13:1). No true doctrine is supported by only one author. This means that if a doctrine like predestination is not confirmed by other writers, one's interpretation of the doctrine is wrong. The correct interpretation will both agree with and be confirmed and supported by other writers of Scripture.

RECOMMENDED READING

Rightly Dividing the Word by Ira L. Milligan. One of God's favorite tactics to hide truth is to place it in plain sight but to disguise it as something other than what it is. Almost all spiritual truth is first clothed with a natural disguise. When we remove the natural covering, we find the naked truth! Like wheat, the natural husk must be removed from the grain before it is usable. *Rightly Dividing the Word* carefully guides the serious Bible student step by step through the Scriptures to safely obtain these hidden treasures. A must-have for serious students of the Word.

Chapter Five

THE MYSTERY OF GODLINESS

For two days I listened attentively as our instructor described the paradigm shift that our society is presently caught up in. It was a leadership seminar—or to be more accurate, a leader-*shift* seminar. Most of us were aware, as our instructor pointed out, that not only is our society undergoing major transition, but our churches are too. We were willing and eager to implement whatever changes we saw necessary to keep abreast of the changing times—although most of us were equally aware that we didn't know exactly how to go about the process. All in all, we were open and receptive to what he was saying.

He taught that we are being challenged by everything from postmodernism to syncretism as the Church ponderously moves into the twenty-first century. Then on the third morning he began describing the great revival that is taking place near and below the equator, especially in the nations of the southern hemisphere. He said one of the revival's key elements is a revelation of the Trinitarian doctrine. At that point he made a rather futile attempt to explain the Trinity. After stumbling for several minutes, he ended his discourse with, "The Trinity is a great mystery! No one fully understands it."

I was genuinely shocked. Here was a highly educated doctor of theology who not only didn't understand the doctrine of the Trinity, apparently he didn't even comprehend the doctrine of mysteries!

THE DOCTRINE OF MYSTERIES

The Bible refers to mysteries over twenty times, starting with Jesus in Mark 4:11, and from the onset it teaches that mysteries are anything but mysterious. They are truths that were once carefully guarded secrets but now are openly revealed to God's children:

> *And* [Jesus] *said to them, "To you it has been given to know the mystery of the kingdom of God; but to those who are outside, all things come in parables"* (Mark 4:11).

When the Bible speaks of mysteries, it isn't speaking of things mysterious and hard to understand. Actually, the exact opposite is true. A mystery is truth that lies hidden within the Old Testament scriptures but is now plainly revealed in the New! For example, in Romans 16:25-26 Paul tells us the gospel was once a mystery but is now, through preaching, made known to all nations:

> *Now to Him who is able to establish you according to my gospel and the preaching of Jesus Christ, according to the revelation of the mystery kept secret since the world began but now made manifest, and by the prophetic*

Scriptures made known to all nations, according to the commandment of the everlasting God, for obedience to the faith.

Another example is found in Ephesians:

Indeed you have heard of the dispensation of the grace of God which was given to me for you, how that by revelation He made known to me the mystery...which in other ages was not made known to the sons of men, as it has now been revealed by the Spirit to His holy apostles and prophets (Ephesians 3:2-3,5).

In this passage Paul tells us the doctrine of grace was once a mystery hidden deep within the Old Testament scriptures, but it is now openly revealed to the apostles and prophets of the New Testament era. Likewise, when the Scriptures speak of *great* mysteries, they aren't speaking of things that are extraordinarily difficult to understand. Instead, they are speaking of truths that are very great—revelations that are very wonderful and important. This is seen in Paul's exposition of the mystery of godliness:

And without controversy great is the mystery of godliness: God was manifested in the flesh, justified in the Spirit, seen by angels, preached among the Gentiles, believed on in the world, received up in glory (1 Timothy 3:16).

THE MYSTERY OF GODLINESS

The mystery of godliness is indeed a *great* mystery, for it goes to the very heart of the Trinitarian doctrine. This doctrine is easily understood and explained—not by trotting out the usual explanations and arguments of modern theologians, but by using a train of reasoning developed by a long-forgotten, humble bishop from the fourth century named Athanasius. And this we will do, but first we need to condense two of the most popular views concerning this doctrine—one pro, the other con—into their basic components.

An oversimplification of the orthodox Trinitarian view is simply that God is one God in three *persons*—God the Father, God the Son, and God the Holy Spirit. These three are coequal and coeternal. Conversely, modalism (or Sabellianism), which was developed and debated in the second and third centuries and revived in the early part of the twentieth century, affirms there is only one God, but God has *manifested* Himself as the Father in creation, the Son in redemption, and the Holy Spirit in sanctification. This view is commonly referred to as *Oneness* and is held by several, but not all, Pentecostal organizations today. Both the orthodox Trinitarian view and the Oneness view are monotheistic, although Oneness adherents (and Muslims) accuse Trinitarians of being polytheist because they think the Trinitarians worship three gods, which Trinitarians readily deny.

Proponents of Oneness are quick to point out that the word *Trinity* isn't in the Bible but was first coined by a lawyer named Tertullian somewhere around A.D. 220. Actually the word was derived from the Greek word *trias,* and was first used by Theophilus approximately fifty years before Tertullian. But Tertullian's writings and his use of the Latin *trinitas* popularized the word and formed the rudimentary teachings that would later develop into the orthodox doctrine.

Obviously, as Church history discloses, being orthodox doesn't automatically prove that a doctrine is true. But a quick sampling of Scripture shows the basis for this doctrine goes back much further than Tertullian or Theophilus. Various aspects of it are found in the Gospels, in almost every New Testament Epistle, and even in several books of the Old Testament. For example, Proverbs 30:4 asks:

Who has ascended into heaven, or descended? Who has gathered the wind in His fists? Who has bound the waters in a garment? Who has established all the ends of the earth? What is His name, and what is His Son's name, if you know?

Jesus appears to be alluding to this scripture when He told Nicodemus, *"No one has ascended to heaven but He who came down from heaven, that is, the Son of Man who is in heaven"* (John 3:13). Another irrefutable illustration of this truth is Paul's beautiful and inspiring blessing ministered to the Corinthians in the parting words of his final letter to them:

The grace of the Lord Jesus Christ, and the love of God, and the communion of the Holy Spirit be with you all. Amen (2 Corinthians 13:14).

And yet another—parts of which are repeated in many of Paul's other Epistles—is Ephesians 1:2-3:

Grace to you and peace from God our Father and the Lord Jesus Christ. Blessed be the God and Father of our

Lord Jesus Christ, who has blessed us with every spiritual blessing in the heavenly places in Christ.

Although opponents of Trinitarianism are in the minority, nevertheless there has to be a reason for their opposition. This debate has raged on for over seventeen hundred years and has filled volumes with arguments from both sides. So rather than add volumes more to it, I will keep this discussion short. Instead of getting into the endless debate over *manifestations* versus *persons* (variously defined as *hypostasis, subsistentia, persona, etc.*), I will approach it from Athanasius's viewpoint and give brief supporting evidence from Scripture as I go.

Athanasius's path to understanding God was simple. He wrote, "Although God Himself is above all, the road which leads to Him is not far, nor even outside ourselves, but is within us."[1] He taught that because people were created in the image and likeness of God, they can comprehend God's divine attributes by examining and recognizing fundamental truths about themselves.

We find this truth echoed in Paul's Epistle to the Romans. Paul declared that people who are ignorant of God and live in unrighteousness are without excuse:

Because that which is known of God is manifest in them; for God manifested it unto them. For the invisible things of him since the creation of the world are clearly seen, being perceived through the things that are made, [even] *his everlasting power and divinity...* (Romans 1:19-20 ASV).

PERCEIVING THE INVISIBLE

Notice that Paul said that God's eternal power and divinity are both seen and perceived through His creation. This revelation has two separate aspects—*divinity* and *power.*

First, we'll address His divinity: in the same way that each person is one, yet consists of three distinct, divisible parts—spirit, soul, and body—likewise, God is divisible into three distinct, separate parts (see 1 Thessalonians 5:23; Hebrews 4:12). The Father corresponds to the soul of a person, the Holy Spirit to the spirit, and the Son to the body.

So, although God is indeed one, and like each person He has only one identity, He has chosen to reveal Himself as He actually exists—an eternal, complex entity composed of Spirit, Soul, and Body! God's Spirit, obviously, is revealed in the various manifestations of the Holy Spirit and is consistent with the human spirit. God's Soul corresponds to the soul of person and is revealed in and through the Father, *"who works all things after the counsel of his own will"* (Ephesians 1:11 KJV). And God's Body is revealed through His only begotten Son, Jesus, whom Paul said is *"the head of the body, the church"* (Colossians 1:18).

The primary debate that has raged through the ages—and still rages—is this: Did God create the Son, or was He always part of, and with, the Father? Is He truly coequal and coeternal, or was there a "time" when He was not? I believe, like Athanasius, that the Logos was always with the Father, and as both John and Paul agree, in the fullness of time He became flesh in the form of the Son and dwelt among us (see John 1:3,14; Galatians 4:4).

If this analysis is correct, then the Logos both was and is God's Body. John 1:1 says, *"In the beginning was the Word* [Greek *logos*], *and the Word was with God, and the Word was God."* In the same way that a person's body is subordinate to his or her soul, yet is equal to and has always been with that person, even so God's body (which was manifest in and through the flesh of His Son) is subordinate to the Father, yet is equal to and has always been a part of God.

This explains the seemingly paradoxical statement Jesus made in John 5:30: *"I can of Myself do nothing…"* (relative to the view that the three persons of the Godhead are coequal). Also, although we are made up of spirit, soul, and body, our bodies as they exist now have an end. Likewise, Jesus said, *"The things concerning Me have an end"* (Luke 22:37).

This view also reveals why Jesus, *"born of a woman, born under the law,"* could be tempted by sin, yet through the Spirit overcome its power and deceptive persuasions and maintain His purity (see Galatians 4:4.) As the Son of Man, He was fallible. As the Son of God, He was victorious over both sin and its evil consequence—death.

This understanding gives us answers to questions such as, was Jesus telling the truth when He said, *"My Father is greater than I"* (John 14:28)? If He was, then He and His Father cannot be the same person, but they can both be *part* of the same person, which is what the Scriptures actually teach.

If Jesus is the Father (which modalism affirms, and if the opponents of Trinitarianism are correct, He has to be), then we need to ask some questions: What did Jesus mean by, *"When you lift up the Son of Man, then you will know that I am He, and that I do nothing of Myself; but as My Father taught Me, I speak these things"* (John 8:28)? If He is the Father, did He teach Himself? If not, why did He say otherwise?

If Jesus is the Father, then His prayers in the Garden of Gethsemane were an insincere farce, designed to deceive instead of being submitted to the Father for the purpose of obtaining help (see Luke 22:42). If Jesus is the Father, instead of being the Son of the Father, in whom the Father dwelled, then He is a deceiver. But we know that Jesus was sincere in all that He said and did. He is, indeed:

> *...The brightness of His glory and the express image of His person, and upholding all things by the word of His power, when He had by Himself purged our sins, sat down at the right hand of the Majesty on high* (Hebrews 1:3).

Oneness adherents' strongest argument supporting Jesus being His own Father is His reply to Philip's request for Him to *"show us the Father."*

> *Philip said to Him, "Lord, show us the Father, and it is sufficient for us." Jesus said to him, "Have I been with you so long, and yet you have not known Me, Philip? He who has seen Me has seen the Father; so how can you say, 'Show us the Father'?"* (John 14:8-9)

Although at first glance it appears the Oneness people have won the debate hands down, it is in appearance only. They happily forget that previously Jesus had scolded the Jews by saying, *"And the Father Himself, who sent Me, has testified of Me. **You have neither heard His voice at any time, nor seen His form**"* (John 5:37). These men were looking at the same man whom Philip saw. If the Jews still had not seen the Father after seeing Jesus, then Philip didn't see the Father by looking at Him either. Jesus revealed the Father through obedience to His will, speaking His word, and performing His works.

When Jesus told Philip, *"He who has seen Me has seen the Father,"* He did not mean that He *was* the Father, but rather that the Father was in Him and had revealed Himself to them through His miraculous power. Jesus told the Jews:

> *If I do not do the works of My Father, do not believe Me; but if I do, though you do not believe Me, believe the works, that you may know and believe that the Father is in Me, and I in Him* (John 10:37-38).

God cannot lie or be tempted with evil, yet the Scriptures teach that Jesus was tempted in all points as we are. Modalism leaves too many questions unanswered to be correct—questions that find their answers easily enough in the doctrine of the Trinity.

KNOWING GOD THROUGH CREATION

Now, let's examine the second aspect of Paul's twofold witness found in his Epistle to the Romans:

> *For the invisible things of him since the creation of the world are clearly seen, being perceived through the things that are made,* [even] *his everlasting **power** and **divinity**...* (Romans 1:20 ASV).

Athanasius, like Paul, taught that it is possible to know God through His creation, which, "As though in written characters, declares in a loud voice, by its order and harmony, its own Lord and Creator."[2] Truly, as the psalmist exclaimed:

The heavens declare the glory of God; and the firmament shows His handiwork. Day unto day utters speech, and night unto night reveals knowledge. There is no speech nor language where their voice is not heard (Psalm 19:1-3).

Paul realized that God's *"everlasting power and divinity"* are revealed in nature in parable form. This is especially true concerning the sun (for this reason, sun worship was predominant in many ancient religions). The sun's seemingly eternal characteristics resemble the Father's, to which Scripture also testifies: *"For the Lord God is a sun..."* (Psalm 84:11). The sun provides light and warmth, ruling over the day even as the moon rules over the night. Under its benevolent gaze plants thrive and grow, providing food and shelter for both humans and beasts. Without the sun, life as we know it could not exist on earth. But the sun's enormous power is useless without some means of conveying it to the earth. This is accomplished by sunlight.

Light's characteristics, like the sun's, show us an important truth about the Trinity. Sunlight is invisible. It proceeds forth from the sun, and is of the same essence as the sun, yet it isn't the sun. If it was the sun, it would destroy us. Instead, it safely transfers the sun's power to us in a way that blesses us. Jesus said of the Holy Spirit, *"...He shall not speak of himself.... He shall glorify me..."* (John 16:13-14 KJV). Similarly, sunlight manifests and glorifies its source and illuminates the objects upon which it shines, but it in itself is invisible.

Finally, both the glory of the sun and its marvelous light would be unknown and unappreciated without the presence of humankind. So it is with God. God's magnificent glory is revealed through the Logos, through which and by which He made the worlds. For, *"The same was in the beginning with God. All things were made by him; and without him was not any thing made that was made"* (John 1:2-3 KJV). This brings us full circle to where we started—back to the mystery of godliness.

THE MYSTERY OF GODLINESS REVEALED

God has seven noncommunicable attributes: He is invisible, immortal, immutable, eternal, omnipotent, omnipresent, and omniscient. Though initially His intentions were a hidden mystery (unperceived by those who originally received the oracles of God), His express purpose in all that He created was to bring glory to Himself by manifesting His divine attributes through weak, fallible flesh. His first son, Adam, who was given authority over all the works of His hands, failed. Adam's failure was according to divine design, for it set the stage for God to be glorified through the Logos (His Word), which in due time became flesh in the form of His only begotten Son and dwelt among us.

Jesus, whom the Father sent to be the Savior of the world, of necessity came in the weakness of human flesh so that

God could be glorified through Him. So, as His intentions were from the beginning:

> *…God was manifested in the flesh* [of His Son], *justified in the Spirit, seen by angels, preached among the Gentiles, believed on in the world,* [and] *received up in glory* (1 Timothy 3:16).

As Paul proclaimed, *"Oh, the depth of the riches both of the wisdom and knowledge of God! How unsearchable are His judgments and His ways past finding out!"* (Romans 11:33).

QUESTIONS AND ANSWERS

1. How can one deny that Jesus is the Father? Didn't Jesus say, *"I and My Father are one"*?

Yes, He did (John 10:30). He also prayed this prayer to the Father, *"And the glory which You gave Me I have given them,* **that they may be one just as We are one"** (John 17:22), showing us that Jesus's concept of being one with the Father doesn't necessitate one inseparable entity.

2. What does the word Godhead mean?

Godhead is an English word used to translate two different, though related, Greek words—the first, *theos* (deity), is found in Acts 17:29, and the second, *theios* (divinity), is used by Paul in his Epistle to the Romans (1:20). *Deity* actually means "a god," whereas *divinity* refers to godlike attributes or characteristics.[3] Jesus was divine in that He fully manifested the Father's attributes, and He was deity in that He was God and not simply godlike. Paul said, *"For in Him dwells all the fullness of the Godhead* [Greek *Theos*] *bodily"* (Colossians 2:9).

3. Are there really three persons in the Godhead?

Whether there are three persons in the Godhead (deity) depends upon how you define *persons*. The Godhead debate has been fraught with problems from the beginning because of the difficulty of using finite terms to describe an infinite God. When using the word *person,* the original framers of the Trinity doctrine did not mean "an individual of specified character" as we mean when we use the word today. The original Latin word was *persona,* which means "the role one assumes or displays in public or society." Three *persons,* as we use the word today, would denote three separate personalities. This is certainly not true of the Spirit, Soul, and Logos of God any more than it is true of the three parts of humans. However, *persona* can refer to different aspects of the same individual's personality, which *is* true of both God and us.

4. Oneness proponents teach that the Logos is God's thoughts, that Jesus existed only in the mind of God before He was begotten and born. They quote Psalm 139:14-17 to prove their point. Is this correct?

If it is, then you will never get to see Jesus. He is now *"where He was before"* (*"What then if you should see the Son of Man ascend where He was before?"*—John 6:62). If Jesus existed only in the mind of God before He was born, then He exists only in His mind now.

Jesus is both *on* the Father's right hand, and He *is* the Father's right hand! In Christ, the Father *"made bare His holy arm"* to save the world (see Isaiah 52:10). He said, *"My righteousness is near; my salvation is gone forth, and mine arms shall judge the people; the isles shall wait upon me, and on mine arm shall they trust"* (Isaiah 51:5 KJV; see also 53:1; 63:5).

The Logos was, and is, God's Body, not just His thoughts. Originally God's body was invisible; then it was made visible in Christ; and at this time it is invisible once more. If you are saved, this same invisible Jesus now dwells in you (see Colossians 1:27).

5. What are postmodernism and syncretism?

In my opinion, the postmodernism that has invaded our society today is simply a revival of ancient humanism. (Humanism is the belief that through education and innate goodness man can save himself.) Postmodernism is society's reaction against earlier modernistic principles, which is usually carried to extremes.

Syncretism is the act of combining different systems of belief. For example, those who say there is good in all of the world's major religions and who attempt to take the best of each and mix them into one homogeneous whole are practicing syncretism.

6. What is Sabellianism and modalism, and where did these terms come from?

Sabellianism is derived from Sabellius, a third-century teacher and exponent of modalism. Modalism refers to separate *modes,* or manifestations, of God, and today finds its expression in Oneness theology.

7. What is monotheism and polytheism?

Monotheism is the belief that there is only one God. Polytheism is the belief that there are many gods. Both Trinitarian and Oneness Christians are monotheistic. Hinduism is one example of polytheism.

RECOMMENDED READING

A History of Christian Thought: Volume I: From the Beginnings to the Council of Chalcedon (Revised Edition) by Justo L. Gonzalez (Abingdon Press, 1987). This book (and its two companions, Volumes II and III) is an indispensable resource for those who are interested in the development of Christian doctrine.

ENDNOTES

1. Justo L. Gonzalez, *A History of Christian Thought, Volume I* (Revised Edition), (Abingdon Press, 1987).

2. Ibid.

3. Strong's.

Chapter Six

THE MYSTERY OF BAPTISMS

Have you ever stood waist deep in freezing water, waiting for a large, icy wave to wash over you? I have! In 1962 I was stationed at a U.S. military base in the Aleutian Islands off the coast of Alaska. While there, I turned my heart and life over to Christ. Soon afterward I expressed my desire to be baptized.

It was a bitter cold, winter morning and our chaplain, a Methodist minister, had already baptized several new converts by sprinkling them with water while we were still in the chapel. About a dozen of us had asked to be immersed, so he took us to the nearest baptistry—which happened to be the Bering Sea! He baptized the other men first, saving me until last. Standing waist deep in the frigid water, he looked a little perplexed, seemingly uncertain of what to say. Unlike the others, I had requested that he baptize me in the same manner the apostles baptized their converts in the Book of Acts.

Watching the waves, he waited for one of sufficient height. As it rolled in, he leaned me over backward so the water would cover me, meanwhile exclaiming, "In Jesus' name." Once released, I hastily waded to the shore where a friend waited for me with a coat and towel. It was the first time that I was baptized in water—and by far the most memorable—but it wasn't the last. Although I now know it wasn't necessary, I was rebaptized later because I wasn't certain the chaplain knew what he was doing!

THE SEVEN BAPTISMS

Water baptism is one of seven individual baptisms introduced in Scripture. As we previously discussed in Chapter Four, although all seven are important, one is indispensable—the baptism of faith. Paul's *"for by grace you have been saved through faith"* is one of the most oft-quoted scriptures in Christendom. Peter agrees with Paul's statement, adding that saving faith is in reality a baptism (see Ephesians 2:8; 1 Peter 3:21). But even though faith is of utmost importance, it is but one of the seven. To be properly equipped, we need to understand them all.

In this chapter we will concern ourselves primarily with the third one on the list—*water baptism*. Although water baptism is by far the most familiar form of baptism, its true meaning and purpose is probably the least known and understood of the seven. But first it may be beneficial to introduce and briefly discuss each type of baptism, which I will do in the order they are normally administered and received.

As we've already mentioned, the first is the baptism of *repentance,* and the second is *faith*. These two actually immerse us into the Kingdom of God. The first separates us from our former sinful lifestyle; the second unites us with God through our Lord Jesus Christ.

The third, water baptism, is the baptism of *separation,* and the fourth is the baptism of the *Spirit.* As we will discuss later, water baptism releases us bodily from the Law of Moses, and the baptism of the Holy Spirit enables and empowers us to be true witnesses of Christ's resurrection. One can readily see that the basic gospel message—the death, burial, resurrection, and witness of the resurrection of Jesus Christ—is administered through these first four baptisms. Although anyone who has been immersed into the first two is a true, born-again believer, Jesus said without the second two we cannot enter the Kingdom of God:

> *Jesus…said, "Most assuredly, I say to you, unless one is born again, he cannot see the kingdom of God."*

> [And,] *"Most assuredly, I say to you, unless one is born of water and the Spirit, he cannot **enter** the kingdom of God"* (John 3:3,5).

Moses was allowed to see the promised land, but he wasn't allowed to enter into it because at a critical time he rebelled and failed to obey God (see Numbers 20:10-12; Deuteronomy 3:27). Likewise, born-again believers can *see* the Kingdom through faith (*"For we walk by faith, not by sight"*—2 Corinthians 5:7). But it is an entirely different matter to actually *experience* its power and glory through the baptism of the Holy Spirit. And everyone should, because every believer has this privilege offered to them—for God promises the gift of the Holy Spirit to everyone who obeys and is baptized in water in Christ's name (see Acts 2:38-39).

The fifth baptism is the long-awaited baptism of fire that John the Baptist prophesied in Luke 3:16-17. Fire baptism actually has "cloven tongues"—that is, it is two baptisms in one—*power* and, as John warned in verse 17, *purification:*

> *John answered, saying to all, "I indeed baptize you with water; but One mightier than I is coming, whose sandal strap I am not worthy to loose. **He will baptize you with the Holy Spirit and fire**. His winnowing fan is in His hand, and He will thoroughly clean out His threshing floor, and gather the wheat into His barn; but the chaff He will burn with unquenchable fire"* (Luke 3:16-17).

The seventh and last—but certainly not the least—is the baptism of *suffering*. This baptism is manifest through the willing sacrifice of the saints. Shortly before going to the cross, Jesus referred to it in His response to James and John's request to be placed on His right and left hands in His glory:

> *But Jesus said to them, "You do not know what you ask. Are you able to drink the cup that I drink, and be baptized with the baptism that I am baptized with?" They said to Him, "We are able." So Jesus said to them, "You will indeed drink the cup that I drink, and with the baptism I am baptized with you will be baptized; but to sit on My right hand and on My left is not Mine to give, but it is for those for whom it is prepared"* (Mark 10:38-40).

SEVEN FOUNDATIONAL DOCTRINES

Each baptism corresponds directly to one of the seven foundational doctrines of Christ which are enumerated in

Hebrews 6:1-2. This passage also shows that the doctrine of baptisms is foundational to the Christian message:

> *Therefore, leaving the discussion of the elementary principles of Christ, let us go on to perfection, not laying again the foundation of repentance from dead works and of faith toward God, of **the doctrine of baptisms**, of laying on of hands, of resurrection of the dead, and of eternal judgment.*

The relationship between the first three doctrines and the first three baptisms is obvious. The fourth doctrine, laying on of hands, is administered by those who are baptized and anointed by the Holy Spirit. Jesus said, *"It is the Spirit who gives life; the flesh profits nothing..."* (John 6:63). For example, when believers lay hands on the sick and they recover, it is God's Spirit who heals them, not the believers themselves (see Mark 16:18; James 5:14-15).

The fifth and sixth doctrines are fulfilled in the two manifestations of the baptism of fire—corresponding to the resurrection of the dead and eternal judgment respectively. God's long-awaited and much-needed resurrection power is necessary before the Church can complete her end-time assignment to publish the gospel to all nations. But the same power that raises the dead will also kill the living, as Ananias and Sapphira suddenly discovered to their dismay (see Acts 5:1-11).

Peter, who administered God's judgment to this infamous couple, assures us that judgment *begins* at the house of God (see 1 Peter 4:17). Before God brings the final judgment upon the wicked of this world, He must first judge His own.

The tares will be removed from the Church before Christ commences pouring fire out upon the earth.

The seventh doctrine, perfection, is accomplished through the baptism of suffering and consists of persecutions and hardships endured for the gospel's sake. Jesus laid down the pattern for us to follow by offering Himself as a willing sacrifice for our sins.

> *Though he were a Son, yet learned he obedience by the things which he suffered; and being made perfect, he became the author of eternal salvation unto all them that obey him* (Hebrews 5:8-9 KJV).

Jesus said, *"Greater love has no one than this, than to lay down one's life for his friends"* (John 15:13).

As one can see, especially by comparing the baptisms to the foundational doctrines of the Church, six of the seven baptisms have a clearly defined meaning and purpose. But what is the reason for baptizing people in water? What purpose does it serve? The answer to these questions lies hidden deep within the Law.

WATER BAPTISM'S SIGNIFICANCE

By comparing the first three baptisms to the basic tenets of the gospel—dying with Christ in repentance, being buried with Him through water baptism, and rising with Him to walk in newness of life through faith in His resurrection—one can see that water baptism corresponds to Christ's burial. Herein lies the key to understanding its significance. Moses wrote:

If a man has committed a sin deserving of death, and he is put to death, and you hang him on a tree, his body shall not remain overnight on the tree, but you shall surely bury him that day, so that you do not defile the land which the Lord your God is giving you as an inheritance; for he who is hanged is accursed of God (Deuteronomy 21:22-23).

Through the Law, every sin results in the curse of death, for *"the soul who sins shall die..."* (Ezekiel 18:20). None are excused, *"for all have sinned and fall short of the glory of God"* (Romans 3:23). Every one of us old enough to read this is under a death sentence unless we have been redeemed by the blood of the Lamb.

After John was put in prison, Jesus came to Galilee, preaching the gospel of the kingdom of God, and saying, *"The time is fulfilled, and the kingdom of God is at hand. Repent, and believe in the gospel"* (Mark 1:14-15).

Though we may be ever so willing to believe and obey, there is one problem. As believers, our *spirits* are ready and willing to believe and serve God. Likewise, our *souls* rejoice at the good news of the gospel and are quite willing to turn from the temporary pleasures of sin and obey the Master. But our *carnal minds* say, "No way, José! I'm not going to surrender my will and give up my pleasures and serve God!"

The Bible doesn't just say the carnal mind *will not*, it says it *cannot* serve God. (*"Because the carnal mind is enmity against God; for it is not subject to the law of God, nor indeed can be"*—Romans 8:7). So, regardless of how willing our spirits may be, and how much our souls acquiesce to our spirits' will, our carnal minds simply cannot agree and go along with the program. Therefore, in the same way that God designed a plan of redemption for our spirits (faith and confession) and our souls (repentance), He has also covered our stubborn and rebellious carnal minds as well (baptism).

Christ saves our spirits by His wonderful gift of grace: *"For by grace you have been saved through faith, and that not of yourselves; it is the gift of God"* (Ephesians 2:8). *"Most assuredly, I say to you, he who believes in Me has everlasting life"* (John 6:47). But what about our souls?

The soul, too, is covered by God's threefold plan of redemption. In essence, our spirits *are saved* through faith in the finished work of Christ. Our souls *are being saved* through repentance and patient continuance in obedience to the gospel (see Hebrews 6:12; 10:39). And, eventually, our bodies *will be saved* by the resurrection of the dead.

After Jesus arose from the dead, He met two men on their way to a village named Emmaus. After He walked some distance with them, He revealed His identity and told them *"that repentance and remission of sins should be preached in His name to all nations, beginning at Jerusalem"* (Luke 24:47). On the day of Pentecost, Peter followed suit by commanding three thousand converts to *"repent, and be baptized every one of you in the name of Jesus Christ for the remission of sins"* (Acts 2:38). Notice that both scriptures specifically state baptism is for the "remission of sins"—but how does water baptism take away sins?

Paul taught that sin was by the Law: *"For until the law sin was in the world, but sin is not imputed when there is no law"* (Romans 5:13). Since sin is imputed by the Law, sin is removed by removing one from under the Law. This is precisely what baptism accomplishes.

When Christ died on the cross, He was accursed of God. In obedience to the Law, He was taken down and buried the same day He died. Likewise, when we die with Him in repentance, we are supposed to be buried too. Paul says that once we are buried with Christ through baptism, we are to reckon ourselves *"to be dead indeed to sin, but alive to God in Christ Jesus our Lord"* (Romans 6:11). Although we have died to this world in our hearts, our bodies are still very much alive and responsive to it. But through baptism we are made free from the Law.

So where does water baptism come into play? Simply this: The Law has dominion over a person as long as he or she lives. If he dies by hanging on a tree, it also has dominion over his carcass until he is buried. Once he is buried, the Law loses all jurisdiction over him. There is no Law governing a resurrected person.

> *Therefore we were buried with Him through baptism into death, that just as Christ was raised from the dead by the glory of the Father, even so we also should walk in newness of life.*

> *For sin shall not have dominion over you, for you are not under law but under grace* (Romans 6:4,14).

One can see, then, that water baptism isn't symbolic; it is an actual burial. This is the reason that baptism in Scripture was always practiced by immersion, never by sprinkling. In fact, the Bible says, *"Now John also was baptizing in Aenon near Salim,* **because there was much water there…"** (John 3:23). It doesn't take "much water" to sprinkle someone, but it does to bury the person's body in obedience to the gospel.

Our hearts are purified and our sins are remitted through faith and repentance. (*"If we confess our sins, He is faithful and just to forgive us our sins and to cleanse us from all unrighteousness"*—1 John 1:9; see also Acts 15:9). However, the human carnal mind cannot be subject to God's Law, and the human physical body cannot believe and repent—it must be delivered from the Law's dominion through burial to be free from the power and penalty of sin.

The necessity of being buried *with* Christ to escape the power of sin also explains why the apostles all baptized in Jesus' name. Paul said, *"And whatever you do in word or deed, do all in the name of the Lord Jesus, giving thanks to God the Father through Him"* (Colossians 3:17; see Acts 2:38; 4:12; 10:43; 19:5).

In response to this you may be asking, "If we are supposed to baptize in Jesus' name, why did Jesus Himself say, *'Go therefore and make disciples of all the nations, baptizing them in the name of the Father and of the Son and of the Holy Spirit'* (Matthew 28:19)?"

First, we need to pay close attention to what Christ actually said. We are to baptize them *"in the **name** of the Father and of the Son and of the Holy Spirit,"* not baptize them using the *titles* Father, Son, and Holy Spirit. So, what is the Father's name?

Jesus said, *"I am come in My Father's name"* (John 5:43). Likewise, when speaking of the promise of the Holy Spirit,

He said, *"Whom the Father will send **in My name**"* (John 14:26). And, as we all know, the Son's name is Jesus. Because the disciples understood that Jesus spoke in a parable (*"All these things Jesus spoke to the multitude in parables..."*— Matthew 13:34), they properly interpreted and obeyed His command and baptized only in His name.

QUESTIONS AND ANSWERS

1. I was taught that water baptism was simply "an outward sign of an inward change." Isn't that right?

No, not altogether right. Water baptism isn't symbolic (a sign). It is a genuine burial of the *old man's* body, by which we lose our citizenship in this world. Paul said, *"Knowing this, that our old man was crucified with Him, that the body of sin might be done away with, that we should no longer be slaves of sin"* (Romans 6:6). Through faith in the spirit, repentance of the soul, and baptism of the body, Christ's cross is applied to our lives and we are released from the carnal ordinances of the Law (see Colossians 2:13-15).

2. Some people teach that since the Bible says water baptism is for the remission of sins, anyone who isn't baptized properly is lost. Is this true or false?

No, it is not true. Jesus said, *"I am the resurrection and the life. He who believes in Me, though he may die, he shall live"* (John 11:25). And Paul said, *"For by grace you have been saved through faith, and that not of yourselves; it is the gift of God"* (Ephesians 2:8). Water baptism has nothing to do with eternal salvation; it has to do with sanctification of the body while we are still active on this earth. Paul said that when we were living in sin, we *"yielded* [our] *members servants to uncleanness and to iniquity unto iniquity,"* but now that we are God's elect, we *"yield* [our] *members servants to righteousness unto holiness...and become servants to God..."* (Romans 6:19,22 KJV).

One of the clearest examples of salvation through faith without the benefit of water baptism is the thief on the cross who confessed Christ as Lord:

> *Then one of the criminals who were hanged blasphemed Him, saying, "If You are the Christ, save Yourself and us." But the other, answering, rebuked him, saying, "Do you not even fear God, seeing you are under the same condemnation? And we indeed justly, for we receive the due reward of our deeds; but this Man has done nothing wrong." Then he said to Jesus,* **"Lord, remember me when You come into Your kingdom."** *And Jesus said to him,* **"Assuredly, I say to you, today you will be with Me in Paradise"** *(Luke 23:39-43).*

3. Some people baptize in the name of the Lord Jesus Christ, and others use Christ's command in Matthew 28:19 as a baptismal formula (*"...baptizing them in the name of the Father and of the Son and of the Holy Spirit"*). Which way is correct?

Those who baptize "in the name of the Lord Jesus Christ" are actually fulfilling the command Jesus gave in Matthew 28:19. From ancient times the Father has been called *Lord,* the Son's name is *Jesus,* and the Holy Spirit is literally the *Christ* (Greek "anointed"). Therefore, when someone says, "I baptize you in the name of the Lord Jesus Christ," that person is both following the example of the apostles and accurately obeying the command of Jesus.

Those who object and say that it is better to do exactly what Jesus said instead of following the apostles' examples and instructions are ignoring the interpretation Jesus Himself gave of His command—*"that repentance and remission of sins should be preached in His name to all nations, beginning at Jerusalem"* (Luke 24:47).

When the proper rules of biblical interpretation are applied to this question, it becomes obvious that baptism is to be administered in Jesus' name and not in the titles of Father, Son, and Holy Spirit. Paul said that every word would be confirmed in the mouth of two or more witnesses, and Matthew's "formula" is *only* found in Matthew 28:19 (see 2 Corinthians 13:1).

4. Didn't the apostles baptize in Jesus' name because they were ministering to the Jews who had previously rejected Christ? Aren't we who believe in Him supposed to baptize in the name of the Father, Son, and Holy Spirit as He said in Matthew 28:19?

No, Peter baptized both Jews *and* Gentiles in Jesus' name, not just Jews. After he preached to Cornelius's household and they were all filled with the Holy Spirit, *"He commanded them to be baptized in the name of the Lord…"* (Acts 10:48). Jesus said *"that repentance and remission of sins should be preached in His name to all nations…"* (Luke 24:47). As the following question and answer shows, Paul also baptized Gentiles in Jesus' name.

5. If I wasn't baptized properly, or if I'm not sure how I was baptized, should I be rebaptized?

Yes, the Scriptures teach that you should. As Jesus said when He was baptized, *"…For thus it is fitting for us to fulfill all righteousness…"* (Matthew 3:15). A biblical example of rebaptism is described in Acts 19. Paul encountered some Gentile disciples on his first trip to Ephesus whom Apollos had baptized improperly out of ignorance:

> *He [Paul] said to them, "Did you receive the Holy Spirit when you believed?" So they said to him, "We have not so much as heard whether there is a Holy Spirit." And he said to them, "Into what then were you baptized?" So they said, "Into John's baptism." Then Paul said, "John indeed baptized with a baptism of repentance, saying to the people that they should believe on Him who would come after him, that is, on Christ Jesus." When they heard this, they were baptized in the name of the Lord Jesus* (Acts 19:2-5).

RECOMMENDED READING

Rightly Dividing the Word by Ira L. Milligan. One of God's favorite tactics to hide truth is to place it in plain sight but disguise it as something other than what it is. Almost all spiritual truth is first clothed with a natural disguise. When we remove the natural covering, we find the naked truth! Like wheat, the natural husk must be removed from the grain before it is usable. *Rightly Dividing the Word* carefully guides the serious Bible student step by step through the Scriptures to safely obtain these hidden treasures. A must-have for serious students of the Word.

Chapter Seven

THE MYSTERY OF THE BRIDE

There are only two mysteries in the Bible specifically called *great*. As the word *great* implies, both these mysteries contain marvelous, in-depth revelations of the *"deep things of God"* (1 Corinthians 2:10). The depth of these two probably surpasses all others. As we saw in Chapter Five, the mystery of godliness not only reveals that God was in Christ reconciling the world unto Himself, but it also shows that manifesting Himself as Savior was His original intention even before He made the worlds. In other words, His wonderful plan of reconciliation was just that—a plan; it wasn't a knee-jerk reaction to Adam's fall.

The second great mystery reveals that all who are reconciled are destined to be Christ's Bride. The question is, and has always been, are we the Bride now, at this present time, or is the marriage set for a future time and place? Before venturing an answer, we need to examine Paul's introduction to this mystery:

> *So husbands ought to love their own wives as their own bodies; he who loves his wife loves himself. For no one ever hated his own flesh, but nourishes and cherishes it,*

just as the Lord does the church. For we are members of
His body, of His flesh and of His bones. "For this reason
a man shall leave his father and mother and be joined
to his wife, and the two shall become one flesh." This is
a great mystery, but I speak concerning Christ and the
church (Ephesians 5:28-32).

Paul's understanding of this mystery appears to be this: God made Eve and presented her to Adam as his bride. They, twain (as a couple), became one flesh. Likewise, God is calling a people out of this world so He can patiently fashion them into Christ's Bride. These called-out ones are the Church. The scripture above clearly establishes that the Church is both Christ's Body and His Bride. But the question remains, when does she become His Bride—now, even as she is being formed, or later, at the marriage supper of the Lamb?

Going back to Ephesians 5:30, Paul said, *"We are members of His body, of His flesh and of His bones,"* meaning we are the Body of Christ now, even as Eve was part of Adam's body. Eve was both Adam's sister (they both had the same Father) and she became his wife. She was also his body (she was made from one of his bones).

Carrying this analogy further, Adam was Eve's head (because he was her husband), even as Christ is the Head of the Church, which is His Body (see 1 Corinthians 11:3; Colossians 1:18). This would indicate that since headship is by marriage, if we are not yet the Bride of Christ, then He is not yet the Head of the Body!

In Second Corinthians 11:2, Paul said, *"For I am jealous over you with godly jealousy: for I have espoused you to one* husband, that I may present you as a chaste virgin to Christ" (KJV). Strong's Concordance says that the word espoused comes from the Greek word harmos, which in this verse means "joined."[1] This is a completely different word than the espoused (mnaomai) of Matthew 1:18:

> Now the birth of Jesus Christ was on this wise: When as his mother Mary was **espoused** [Greek *engaged*] to Joseph, before they came together [i.e., *not yet joined*], she was found with child of the Holy Ghost (KJV).

This concept of being *joined* is paramount to this discussion because Paul said, *"He who is joined to the Lord is one spirit with Him"* (1 Corinthians 6:17). In the same way that Adam and Eve became one flesh through natural union, Christ and the Church become one spirit through spiritual union. This is what Paul refers to when he compares a husband and wife's relationship to Christ and His relationship with the Church, which he calls a great mystery.

HIDDEN SHADOWS

At this point it will be advantageous to go over the principles of *mysteries* again. As we discussed in Chapter Five, mysteries are truths hidden within the Old Covenant but revealed under the New. Mysteries are hidden several different ways, but the two most common are *parables* and *shadows*. Some mysteries are contained in shadows. Hebrews 10:1 says that shadows are *"not the very image of the things,"* which means they are not exact reproductions but are more like dark reflections of the substances they depict. Therefore, sometimes one has to look closely to fully comprehend everything these mysteries reveal.

This is especially true concerning the mystery of the Bride. Under the Old Covenant, God recognized Jerusalem as His wife, and her citizens as daughters (Jerusalem is where He placed His name—see Deuteronomy 12:5; 1 Kings 8:29). In Isaiah 54:5, God assured Israel, *"Your Maker is your husband…."* Similarly, when the Israelites sinned He chided them, *"Where is the bill of your mother's divorcement, whom I have put away?"* (Isaiah 50:1 KJV). Since they could not produce it, Jerusalem was still His wife and He still considered her citizens His children. Paul explains this allegory in Galatians, and the writer of Hebrews shows that New Jerusalem corresponds to the Church:

> *For it is written that Abraham had two sons: the one by a bondwoman, the other by a freewoman. But he who was of the bondwoman was born according to the flesh, and he of the freewoman through promise, which things are symbolic. For these are the two covenants: the one from Mount Sinai which gives birth to bondage, which is Hagar—for this Hagar is Mount Sinai in Arabia, and corresponds to Jerusalem which now is, and is in bondage with her children—but the Jerusalem above is free, which is the mother of us all* (Galatians 4:22-26).

> *But you have come to Mount Zion and to the city of the living God, the heavenly Jerusalem, to an innumerable company of angels, to the general assembly and church of the firstborn who are registered in heaven, to God*

the Judge of all, to the spirits of just men made perfect (Hebrews 12:22-23).

A natural mountain, where the Old Covenant was made; a natural city, with its throne and temple; and a natural kingdom; these composed God's first wife. A spiritual mountain, where the New Covenant is established; a heavenly city and heavenly throne, with a spiritual temple; and a spiritual Kingdom; these compose His second wife, which is the Church.

Marriage is a covenant. God "married" Israel when He gave her the Ten Commandments on Mount Sinai. Since God and His Word are one, when Israel accepted the Commandments, she accepted God as her husband (see John 1:1; Deuteronomy 27:26, Jeremiah 31:32). If this were not true, God would have been committing fornication when He overshadowed the virgin Mary to impregnate her with His only begotten Son! (Mary was an Israelite, therefore she was legally married to God through the Law.)

Also, if this were not true, Israel could not have been guilty of committing adultery against God, as she so often was. A woman must be married to a man before she can commit adultery against him. Likewise, the Church could not be adulterers and adulteresses if we weren't married to Christ (*"Adulterers and adulteresses! Do you not know that friendship with the world is enmity with God?"*—see James 4:4).

So when does this marriage take place? When do we actually become Christ's Bride? When we, from the heart, confess Jesus as Lord, we enter into covenant with Him, and through that covenant we are joined to Him in Spirit—at that point we become His spiritual Bride and citizens of His spiritual Kingdom.

THE LAW OF A HUSBAND

One of the strongest proofs of all that we are the Bride of Christ is found in Romans 7:1-4. (As you read this scripture, remember the Law commanded a widow to marry her husband's brother if her husband died childless—see Deuteronomy 25:5; Matthew 22:24):

> *Know ye not, brethren, (for I speak to them that know the law,) how that the law hath dominion over a man as long as he lives? For the woman which hath an husband is bound by the law to her husband so long as he lives; but if the husband be dead, she is loosed from the law of her husband. So then if, while her husband lives, she be married to another man, she shall be called an adulteress: but if her husband be dead, she is free from that law; so that she is no adulteress, though she be married to another man. Wherefore, my brethren, ye also are become dead to the law by the body of Christ; that ye should be married to another, even to him who is raised from the dead, that we should bring forth fruit unto God* (Romans 7:1-4 KJV).

In this scripture Paul tells us the Law's first wife, Israel, did not bring forth any *living* offspring (until Christ's death and resurrection no one had eternal life). When a man died without a living heir, his wife was commanded to marry his brother to raise up seed in his name. When Christ (who was the Law made flesh) died, the carnal commandments of the Law died, releasing Israel to marry again. But she must marry her first husband's brother to raise up seed to his name. In this case, her dead husband's brother is the risen Christ! In this amazing allegory, Paul shows that Christ figuratively became His own brother when He rose from the dead. Thus, the risen Christ is Israel's second husband (though He is the only the second husband of those Israelites who enter into covenant with Him).

There is only one plan of salvation, so if the Israelites become Christ's Bride when they accept Him as Lord, so do we. We are "grafted in" Israelites (see Romans 11:17-18). Now let us look once more at Paul's exposition of this mystery, in its entirety.

> *Wives, submit yourselves unto your own husbands, as unto the Lord. For the husband is the head of the wife, even as Christ is the head of the church: and he is the savior of the body. Therefore as the church is subject unto Christ, so let the wives be to their own husbands in every thing.*

> *Husbands, love your wives, even as Christ also loved the church, and gave himself for it; that he might sanctify and cleanse it with the washing of water by the word, that he might present it to himself a glorious church, not having spot, or wrinkle, or any such thing; but that it should be holy and without blemish. So ought men to love their wives as their own bodies. He that loves his wife loves himself. For no man ever yet hated his own flesh; but nourishes and cherishes it, even as the Lord*

the church: for we are members of his body, of his flesh, and of his bones. For this cause shall a man leave his father and mother, and shall be joined unto his wife, and they two shall be one flesh. This is a great mystery: but I speak concerning Christ and the church (Ephesians 5:22-32 KJV).

This passage of Scripture plainly shows the Church as Christ's Bride. Paul saw the hidden mystery of the Bride in the Law, and it is this mystery that he emphasized here more than the actual relationship of husbands and wives. So when do we become Christ's Bride? When we accept Him as Lord. In the natural, we marry by making a covenant. Likewise, we are saved by a covenant, and when we make that covenant we are actually marrying Christ in spirit, for *"he who is joined to the Lord is one spirit with Him"* (1 Corinthians 6:17).

THE MARRIAGE SUPPER OF THE LAMB

Where did the question concerning the Church as the Bride originate? In part, it arose from one of the most beautiful prophecies in the Bible—John's description of the marriage supper of the Lamb:

Let us be glad and rejoice, and give honor to him: for the marriage of the Lamb is come, and his wife hath made herself ready. And to her was granted that she should be arrayed in fine linen, clean and white: for the fine linen is the righteousness of saints. And he saith unto me, Write, Blessed are they which are called unto the marriage supper of the Lamb... (Revelation 19:7-9 KJV).

The controversy comes from confusing the festive occasion described here with the actual marriage ceremony that takes place earlier (which, in our case, occurs when we accept Christ as Lord). In verse 7, *wife* in the Greek means exactly that—a woman who is already married. In the Jewish culture a wedding was followed by a feast, which was accompanied with wine and dancing, as when Jesus made wine at the wedding in Cana (see John 2:1-11). The Jews in those days did not just serve refreshments to the guests as our custom is; they had a feast that lasted for seven days. It is this feast (supper) that John saw, not the initial ceremony. So, all who are saved are married to Christ, and at the appointed time they will experience the glorious reception John described above.

Natural marriage is a "shadow" of Christ's spiritual marriage with the Church and not the exact image. Shadows portray rather blurred pictures—though this one is a very beautiful picture—of the substances that make them. Also, Jewish wedding customs were different from ours. This explains one reason Gentiles have a difficult time understanding the parables Jesus told relating to the Church and the Bride.

God often uses different aspects of certain deeds and customs to reveal different portions of truth. As we discussed in Chapter Two, Jesus compared His Second Coming to the actions of a thief. This does not prove that Jesus is a thief! He is not coming to steal. He is coming for those who are already His. This explains the paradoxes and apparent contradictions sometimes encountered when searching parables and shadows for hidden mysteries.

For example, opponents of the Church as the Bride point to the parable of the ten virgins to prove their point. In this parable, the groom is returning from a journey to marry his fiancée:

> *Then the kingdom of heaven shall be likened to ten virgins who took their lamps and went out to meet the bridegroom. Now five of them were wise, and five were foolish. Those who were foolish took their lamps and took no oil with them, but the wise took oil in their vessels with their lamps. But while the bridegroom was delayed, they all slumbered and slept. And at midnight a cry was heard: "Behold, the bridegroom is coming; go out to meet him!"*

> *Watch therefore, for you know neither the day nor the hour in which the Son of Man is coming* (Matthew 25:1-6,13).

As one can see, Jesus's reference in this parable is identical to when He compared Himself to a thief. Both parables use common acts and customs to portray a specific truth—in this case, that His coming is going to be sudden and unexpected.

A *REAL* MYSTERY

Looking again at the allegory Paul used in Galatians 4:21-31, he said, *"Jerusalem which is above…is the mother of us all"* (Galatians 4:26 KJV). The Jerusalem of the Old Testament represents Israel under the Law, but heavenly Jerusalem is the Church:

> *But ye are come unto mount Sion, and unto the city of the living God, the heavenly Jerusalem, and to an innumerable company of angels, to the general assembly and church of the firstborn, which are written in heaven, and to God the Judge of all, and to the spirits of just men made perfect, and to Jesus the mediator of the new covenant, and to the blood of sprinkling, that speaks better things than that of Abel* (Hebrews 12:22-24 KJV).

In Genesis 3:20, Adam called his wife *Eve* because in the natural she is the mother of all "living." Likewise, Christ's wife, the Church, is the mother of all who are spiritually alive. That is the reason Israel had to marry the risen Christ—the Law could not produce any "living" offspring for God!

So we marry Christ, receive His "seed" (which is His Word), and bring forth His likeness in every convert we make. Jesus once asked:

> …*"Who is My mother and who are My brothers?" And He stretched out His hand toward His disciples and said, "Here are My mother and My brothers! For whoever does the will of My Father in heaven is My brother and sister and mother"* (Matthew 12:48-50).

His disciples who do the Father's will are the Church. The conclusion? The Church is Christ's Bride. And as she brings forth His children, who are members of His Body, she is also His mother! Now *that* is a *real* mystery!

QUESTIONS AND ANSWERS

1. What are the consequences of believing the Church isn't Christ's Bride?

This doctrine is especially important in combating the error of the "eternal security" heresy. It explains the primary reason God will reject certain people who were at one time saved (married to Him) but who fell away. The only biblical justification for divorce is adultery. When Christians break their marriage covenant with Christ by committing spiritual adultery and they fail to repent when confronted with the truth (being convicted in their conscience by the Holy Spirit), He divorces them.

2. How does one commit spiritual adultery?

By becoming too friendly with this present world, a condition commonly described as "worldliness":

Adulterers and adulteresses! Do you not know that friendship with the world is enmity with God? Whoever therefore wants to be a friend of the world makes himself an enemy of God (James 4:4).

Many who flirt with the world fall in love with it and are entangled thereby. Jesus warned of this danger in His discourse on the last days. He described the end as a time when *"...lawlessness will abound,* [and] *the love of many will grow cold"* (Matthew 24:12; see also 1 John 2:15-17).

3. Are Israelites who died before Jesus came, such as Abraham and Daniel, also part of the Bride?

Yes. Christ has only one Bride. Paul said, *"And that He might reconcile them both* [Jews and Gentiles] *to God in one body through the cross..."* (Ephesians 2:16). No one is saved by the Law. All who are saved, regardless of what time period they lived in—whether before, during, or after the Law—are saved by faith through the atoning blood of Jesus Christ. *"...Once at the end of the ages,* [Christ] *has appeared to put away sin by the sacrifice of Himself"* (Hebrews 9:26).

In the same way that we look *back* to the cross of Christ, those who came before Jesus looked *forward* to the cross (see Hebrews 11:27).

RECOMMENDED READING

Backgrounds of Early Christianity by Everett Ferguson (William B. Eerdmans Publishing Co., 2003) is without equal in explaining the customs and culture of early Christianity.

ENDNOTE

1. *Strong's Exhaustive Concordance*, Greek #718/719.

For whom the Lord loves He chastens, and scourges every son whom He receives (Hebrews 12:6).

Chapter Eight

SIN, SICKNESS, AND CHASTISEMENT

After ministering and turning the service back over to the pastor, I patiently waited while he closed the service and dismissed the congregation. He then turned and approached me with a scowl on his face. "I don't agree with your doctrine!" he snarled.

Startled, I asked, "Which one?" As far as I knew, I hadn't addressed anything controversial in my message, so I was puzzled as to what he had found so objectionable.

"God won't chastise you by making you sick," he growled.

"How do you explain the scripture in Acts chapter thirteen where Paul smote a man with blindness, telling him, *'The hand of the Lord is upon you, and you shall be blind, not seeing the sun for a time'*? Blindness sure seems like sickness to me!" I replied (see Acts 13:11). "Also, what about First Corinthians chapter eleven? Paul told the Corinthians that because they weren't taking Communion in a worthy manner, some were weak and sick among them, and many had even died! He said if we don't judge ourselves, then God will judge us and chasten us so that we won't be condemned with the world. How do you explain those scriptures?" I asked (see 1 Corinthians 11:29-32).

His reply shocked me even more than his objection to the portion of my message where I referred to God's chastisements. He said, *"I just put those scriptures on the shelf."*

I couldn't believe what I was hearing! How do you reason with a person who takes scriptures that disagree with a specific position and "puts them upon the shelf"? I wondered.

He continued, "I figure that if we are healed by Jesus's stripes, then God won't put sickness upon us. That's the devil's job."

I agreed with him that indeed, sickness is the devil's job—but who gave him the job? When I asked this pastor how God chastens those who sin, he said, "With His Word." His answer was partly right, but he willingly ignored (placed upon the shelf) the rest of what the Scriptures teach about God's chastisements.

God is immutable. The Bible declares that He cannot change or lie. Concerning this matter He said:

Now see that I, even I, am He, and there is no God besides Me; I kill and I make alive; I wound and I heal; nor is there any who can deliver from My hand (Deuteronomy 32:39).

And Paul said, *"If anyone defiles the temple of God, God will destroy him..."* (1 Corinthians 3:17). It doesn't get any plainer than that! To categorically declare, "God won't make you sick" is a direct refutation of what He says about Himself!

Such denial is as narrow-minded as those who teach, "If you are sick, you've sinned." Either extreme is wrong.

Although the Scriptures state that God does not *willingly* afflict or grieve people, it doesn't say that He *won't* afflict them (see Lamentations 3:33). Sometimes affliction is necessary. The writer of Hebrews shows us there are times when God has no other choice:

> And you have forgotten the exhortation which speaks to you as to sons: "My son, do not despise the chastening of the Lord, nor be discouraged when you are **rebuked** by Him; for whom the Lord loves He chastens, and **scourges** [Greek *flogs*] every son whom He receives." If you endure chastening, God deals with you as with sons; for what son is there whom a father does not chasten? But if you are without chastening, of which all have become partakers, then you are illegitimate and not sons.

> Furthermore, we have had human fathers who corrected us, and we paid them respect. Shall we not much more readily be in subjection to the Father of spirits and live? For they indeed for a few days chastened us as seemed best to them, but He for our profit, that we may be partakers of His holiness. Now no chastening seems to be joyful for the present, but **painful**; nevertheless, afterward it yields the peaceable fruit of righteousness to those who have been trained by it (Hebrews 12:5-11).

Initially, when we fall into sin, God deals with us in three stages: First, He patiently gives us "space to repent" (see Ecclesiastes 8:11; Revelation 2:21-22; Romans 2:4). If, after waiting, we still don't show any signs of change, as the pastor referred to above rightly stated, He rebukes us. If we repent and *"…confess our sins, He is faithful and just to forgive us our sins and to cleanse us from all unrighteousness"* (1 John 1:9). But if we harden our hearts and refuse to repent, He steps up the heat—He scourges us.

THREE STEPS OF CORRECTION

In First Corinthians 11:30, Paul shows us that God's painful scourging also consists of three distinct, separate steps: First, God weakens our hands so that our enemies begin to prevail over us. This weakness may manifest itself in any number of ways, including emotional depression, financial problems, social trouble—whatever it takes. If that isn't sufficient to bring about repentance, His next step is to send major trouble, including sickness and disease. If we still harden our hearts and continue in sin, His third and final step is to—reluctantly—send us to the grave.

God's ways never change. This three-step process of chastisement is seen in His dealings with the Israelites throughout the Old Testament. For example, in Hosea 5:10-15, when both the northern kingdom (represented by Ephraim, the largest of the ten tribes) and the southern kingdom (consisting of the tribes of Judah and Benjamin) fell into idolatry, God warned them that He would be unto Ephraim as a moth and unto Judah as rottenness. If that didn't work, He promised that He would be unto Ephraim as a lion and as a young lion unto Judah, tearing and rending them in His fury. If they still didn't turn from idolatry, He would go away and leave them unto themselves—which is the worst possible scenario of all—man destroying man. When faced with this latter possibility, David wisely cried out, *"I am in great distress. Please let us fall into the hand of the Lord, for His mercies are great; but do not let me fall into the hand of man"* (2 Samuel 24:13-14).

COVENANT BENEFITS

Although His reason for using sickness as a rod of correction is clear enough, we may still question how God can legitimately make His children sick when one of His covenant benefits is healing. Psalm 103:2-3 declares, *"Bless the Lord, O my soul, and forget not all His benefits: who forgives all your iniquities, who heals all your diseases."* God even promised to heal His people while they were still under the Law:

> *So you shall serve the Lord your God, and He will bless your bread and your water. And I will take sickness away from the midst of you* (Exodus 23:25).

> *And the Lord will take away from you all sickness, and will afflict you with none of the terrible diseases of Egypt which you have known, but will lay them on all those who hate you* (Deuteronomy 7:15).

As one can see from examining the two scriptures above, healing is part of the Old Covenant. But all covenants, including both the Old and the New, are conditional.

The New Covenant, which is the gospel, provides a "hedge" that protects us on every front, as long as we are faithful to abide by its terms. But every benefit afforded to us through the gospel is conditional, including the benefit of healing. If we fail to keep covenant, we open the door for Satan to come in and take away our promised blessings. (At this point we need to interject that all sickness and disease isn't caused by sin, nor is Satan always the author of sickness. There is more than one source, or cause, of sickness and disease.)

As we conceded earlier, it's the devil's job to make people sick, but usually he can only do so when God affords him the privilege. And when God does, God takes credit for whatever He allows the devil to do. When Satan conspired against Job, he couldn't touch him without first obtaining permission. After Job's initial affliction:

> *Then the Lord said to Satan, "Have you considered My servant Job, that there is none like him on the earth, a blameless and upright man, one who fears God and shuns evil? And still he holds fast to his integrity,* ***although you incited Me against him, to destroy him without cause"*** *(Job 2:3).*

The same concept is also found in the New Testament. Jesus informed Peter:

> *…"Simon, Simon! Indeed, Satan has asked for you, that he may sift you as wheat. But I have prayed for you, that your faith should not fail; and when you have returned to Me, strengthen your brethren" (Luke 22:31-32).*

EXAMINE YOURSELVES

So, if we get sick, how can we tell if it is God's chastisement or simply an attack from our archenemy? The answer is by careful introspection and self-examination. Usually our consciences are enough to inform us if sin is present. To avoid chastisement, Paul advised the Corinthians before taking Communion to *"let* [each] *man examine himself"* (1 Corinthians 11:28). When you check your heart, if your conscience isn't clear, repent. Once you know that your conscience is clear, you can believe God for your healing or whatever else you may need. John assured us:

> *For if our heart condemns us, God is greater than our heart, and knows all things. Beloved, if our heart does not condemn us, we have confidence toward God. And whatever we ask we receive from Him, because we keep His commandments and do those things that are pleasing in His sight* (1 John 3:20-22).

Likewise, James puts self-examination, confession of sin, and forgiveness in the same context with faith for healing. He said:

> *Is anyone among you sick? Let him call for the elders of the church, and let them pray over him, anointing him with oil in the name of the Lord. And the prayer of faith will save the sick, and the Lord will raise him up. And if he has committed sins, he will be forgiven.* **Confess your trespasses to one another, and pray for one another, that you may be healed**... (James 5:14-16).

Trying to have faith with a condemned conscience is like trying to mix oil and water. They are completely incompatible. But some of the worst sins of all don't always register with the conscience. For example, a person's conscience is incapable of warning him or her of inherited sin and its evil consequence because it has no knowledge of it (see Leviticus 26:39-42; Deuteronomy 28:59). Likewise, when someone trespasses against us, we have reason to feel offended, so we usually are not quick to forgive, and so our consciences are often silent in those cases too. Yet being unloving and unforgiving is one of the worst possible traps to fall into. It swings the door wide open to Satan to afflict us with grief.

In the parable of the unmerciful servant, Jesus said those who refuse to forgive others would be "delivered to the tormentors" (see Matthew 18:23-35 KJV). The Bible lists several possible "torments." One is fear. John said, "Fear involves torment" (see 1 John 4:18). Anxiety attacks are often rooted in this behavior. To obtain mercy we must be merciful. Being unforgiving is simply unforgivable—sooner or later it always leads to chastisement. Likewise, as anyone who has ever suffered from migraines will attest, another form of torment is headaches. Although all headaches certainly aren't the result of chastisement, some are (see Jeremiah 30:23).

And lastly, one of the worst offenses that opens the door for Satan's attack is occult practices. In fact, playing with a Ouija board or tarot cards or going to a fortune-teller does more than open the door; these practices actually invite Satan in! Beware, if he is invited in, he will take whatever riches you have available—your health included.

THE FATHER'S WILL

One may ask, "Doesn't the fact that Jesus healed everyone when He ministered to the multitudes prove that it is the Father's will for everyone to be healed?" (*"And the whole multitude sought to touch Him, for power went out from Him and healed them all"*—Luke 6:19). With few exceptions, the answer is *yes!* (The primary exception being those who have lived their lives to the fullest and are ready to go to their reward—see Second Kings 13:14; Hebrews 9:27.) Normally, it is God's will for everyone to be healed. John said, *"Beloved, I pray that you may prosper in all things and be in health, just as your soul prospers"* (3 John 1:2).

The principle point here is God always puts soul prosperity above health and wealth. When we are in sin, our souls aren't prospering very well. So, God may send pressure from financial problems or afflict us with sickness and disease to get our attention so that we will hearken to His corrections.

Paul summed up God's purposes in His dealings with us, *"Now the purpose of the commandment is love from a pure heart, from a good conscience, and from sincere faith"* (1 Timothy 1:5). Love freely forgives, a clear conscience indicates both integrity and proper moral and spiritual conduct, and sincere faith is the precious benefit of both. Now, that's *real* prosperity!

QUESTIONS AND ANSWERS

1. What are some of the ways that God talks to us when He is dealing with us about sin?

The first defense against sin is the conscience. It is always present, and though fallible, if we will listen to it, its nudging is usually sufficient to prevent us from falling into sin's trap. When our consciences are incapable of warning us, God often uses dreams as His next method of communication, as in Job 33:14-19 (KJV):

> *For God speaks once, yea twice, yet man perceives it not. In a dream, in a vision of the night, when deep sleep falls upon men, in slumberings upon the bed; then he opens the ears of men, and seals their instruction, that he may withdraw man from his [own] purpose, and hide pride from man. He keeps back his soul from the pit, and his life from perishing by the sword. He is chastened also with pain upon his bed, and the multitude of his bones with strong pain.*

As you can see from this scripture, when we fail to hear His rebuke, He reverts to sickness. The good news is, if and when we do hear and heed His correction, He follows through with healing and righteousness:

> *If there be a messenger with him, an interpreter, one among a thousand, to show unto man [God's] uprightness: then he is gracious unto him, and saith, Deliver him from going down to the pit: I have found a ransom. His flesh shall be fresher than a child's: he shall return to the days of his youth: he shall pray unto God, and he will be favorable unto him: and he shall see his face with joy: for he will render unto man his righteousness* (Job 33:23-26 KJV).

2. Are there any biblical examples of God using sickness to chastise His people?

Yes, several: Elisha's servant, Gehazi, was smitten with leprosy because of his sin of covetousness (see 2 Kings 5:25-27). Likewise, King Uzziah transgressed by entering the Lord's temple and burning incense. He became angry when the priests rebuked him and was immediately smitten with leprosy (see 2 Chronicles 26:16-19; also 2 Kings 1:2-4; 2 Chronicles 21:12-15).

Another instance worth mentioning is King Asa. The story starts in Second Chronicles chapter 14 and continues all the way through chapter 16, so it is too long to quote the entire text here. To summarize, Asa rebelled against God's prophet when he was rebuked by him. The result was disastrous. Because Asa hardened his heart and refused to repent, he died under God's chastising hand. Below are several excerpts from the story:

> *And at that time Hanani the seer came to Asa king of Judah, and said to him: "Because you have relied on the king of Syria, and have not relied on the Lord your God, therefore the army of the king of Syria has escaped from your hand."*
>
> *Then Asa was angry with the seer, and put him in prison, for he was enraged at him because of this. And Asa oppressed some of the people at that time.*
>
> *And in the thirty-ninth year of his reign, Asa became diseased in his feet, and his malady was severe; yet in*

his disease he did not seek the Lord, but the physicians (2 Chronicles 16:7,10,12).

3. Is there a connection between Asa's sin and the fact that he was diseased in his feet?

Yes, there is. Your feet represent your walk. You walk with your words. If your words are stout against God, as Asa discovered, often your feet suffer the consequence (see Genesis 3:8-9; Acts 9:5).

4. Are there any examples of God using sickness to chastise and execute judgment upon people in the New Testament?

Yes, not only sickness but also death:

But a certain man named Ananias, with Sapphira his wife, sold a possession. And he kept back part of the proceeds, his wife also being aware of it, and brought a certain part and laid it at the apostles' feet. But Peter said, "Ananias, why has Satan filled your heart to lie to the Holy Spirit and keep back part of the price of the land for yourself? While it remained, was it not your own? And after it was sold, was it not in your own control? Why have you conceived this thing in your heart? You have not lied to men but to God." Then Ananias, hearing these words, fell down and breathed his last. So great fear came upon all those who heard these things (Acts 5:1-5).

Another example, also found in Acts, is God's judgment upon Herod after he killed James, threatened Peter, and then glorified himself before the people:

> *So on a set day Herod, arrayed in royal apparel, sat on his throne and gave an oration to them. And the people kept shouting, "The voice of a god and not of a man!" Then immediately an angel of the Lord struck him, because he did not give glory to God. And he was eaten by worms and died* (Acts 12:21-23).

5. Didn't Paul command the Corinthians to turn someone who was sinning over to Satan for the destruction of the flesh?

Yes, a member of the Corinthian church was in incest (probably with his stepmother).

> *It is actually reported that there is sexual immorality among you, and such sexual immorality as is not even named among the Gentiles—that a man has his father's wife!*
>
> *Deliver such a one to Satan for the destruction of the flesh, that his spirit may be saved in the day of the Lord Jesus* (1 Corinthians 5:1,5).

Sexual immorality carries with it an automatic death sentence! Putting verses of Scripture together, we have the following admonition and warning:

> *Flee sexual immorality. Every sin that a man does is outside the body, but **he who commits sexual immorality sins against his own body.***

If anyone defiles the temple of God, God will destroy him. *For the temple of God is holy, which temple you are* (1 Corinthians 6:18; 1 Corinthians 3:17).

RECOMMENDED READING

The Hidden Power of Covenant—Releasing the Fullness of the Blessing of the Gospel of Jesus Christ by Ira L. Milligan. This book reveals the many promises of the New Covenant and the necessary conditions for their fulfillment.

Chapter Nine

THE LAW OF JEALOUSY

Paul's instructions to the Corinthian church to deliver an errant member who had fallen into sexual immorality *"to Satan for the destruction of the flesh, that his spirit may be saved in the day of the Lord Jesus"* is probably one of the strangest and least understood commands in Scripture (see 1 Corinthians 5:5). If and when the need ever exists, how does one actually turn a person over to Satan for destruction anyway? Does anyone know?

The answer is a surprising *yes!* In fact, the answer is found in the scriptures immediately following the command:

> ***Therefore purge out the old leaven***, *that you may be a new lump, since you truly are unleavened. For indeed Christ, our Passover, was sacrificed for us. Therefore **let us keep the feast**, not with old leaven, nor with the leaven of malice and wickedness, but with the unleavened bread of sincerity and truth* (1 Corinthians 5:7-8).

When a person properly "keeps the feast" of Communion, which is the New Testament equivalent of the Old Testament Passover, one of two things happen—either one is judged, justified, and if needed, healed, or one is judged, condemned, and brought under God's chastisement. On the same night that Jesus was betrayed He celebrated the feast of Passover with His disciples. Paul relates the occasion in First Corinthians 11:23-34:

> For I received from the Lord that which I also delivered to you: that the Lord Jesus on the same night in which He was betrayed took bread; and when He had given thanks, He broke it and said, "Take, eat; this is My body which is broken for you; do this in remembrance of Me." In the same manner He also took the cup after supper, saying, "This cup is the new covenant in My blood. This do, as often as you drink it, in remembrance of Me." For as often as you eat this bread and drink this cup, you proclaim the Lord's death till He comes.

> Therefore whoever eats this bread or drinks this cup of the Lord in an unworthy manner will be guilty of the body and blood of the Lord. But let a man examine himself, and so let him eat of the bread and drink of the cup. For he who eats and drinks in an unworthy manner eats and drinks judgment to himself, not discerning the Lord's body. For this reason many are weak and sick among you, and many sleep.

> For if we would judge ourselves, we would not be judged. But when we are judged, we are chastened by the Lord, that we may not be condemned with the world. Therefore, my brethren, when you come together to eat, wait for one another…lest you come together for judgment….

But how did Paul know that taking Communion would bring judgment upon the unworthy? Where did he obtain his information? Because the New Testament is the Old Testament revealed, his intriguing revelation had to come directly from the Old Testament scriptures—which, without question, it did.

In Exodus 11:4–12:14, God told Moses to warn Israel that an angel of death would soon pass through the land and *"all the firstborn of the land of Egypt shall die"* (see Exodus 11:5). Protection would be afforded to the Israelites, but only if they followed God's instructions to the letter. To escape death, each household had to acquire an unblemished lamb and kill it at twilight on the fourteenth day of the month, placing the lamb's blood on the doorpost of the house. Moses instructed them to roast and eat the lamb *"…with a belt on your waist, your sandals on your feet, and your staff in your hand. So you shall eat it in haste. It is the Lord's Passover"* (Exodus 12:11).

> *For I will pass through the land of Egypt on that night, and will strike all the firstborn in the land of Egypt, both man and beast; and against all the gods of Egypt I will execute judgment: I am the Lord. Now the blood shall be a sign for you on the houses where you are.* ***And when I see the blood, I will pass over you****; and the plague shall not be on you to destroy you when I strike the land of Egypt.* ***So this day shall be to you a memorial****; and you shall keep it as a feast to the Lord throughout your generations.* ***You shall keep it as a feast by an everlasting ordinance*** *(Exodus 12:12-14).*

In the Old Testament, God instituted the annual Passover feast to continually remind Israel that He miraculously delivered them from Egyptian slavery. He proclaimed it an "everlasting ordinance." Similarly, in the New Testament, He instituted Communion to remind us that He mercifully delivered us from sin through the precious blood of the spotless Lamb of God—His only begotten Son.

Jesus was dying on the cross to atone for our sins at the same time the Israelite priests were killing the Passover lambs to atone for the sins of Israel—although *"it is not possible that the blood of bulls and goats* [or sheep] *could take away sins"* (Hebrews 10:4). Nevertheless, before one can fully understand and appreciate Communion, one must first understand Passover and its related ordinance, the "law of jealousy." (This law was an *"offering of jealousy, an offering for remembering, for bringing iniquity to remembrance"*—see Numbers 5:14-29.)

THE BENEFITS OF COMMUNION

As we mentioned previously, when Communion is taught and administered properly, it either heals the saints or makes them weak or sick—when necessary, even unto death. This is comparable to how Passover healed the Israelites while at the same time raining death and destruction down upon the Egyptians. Similarly, the law of jealousy brought sickness or conception, whichever was appropriate at the time the jealousy offering was administered. We'll examine these two ordinances and their effects upon the Israelites as we continue.

First, the good news! Psalm 105:37 declares that when Israel first came out of Egypt, *"...There was none feeble among His tribes."* Obviously, God strengthened and healed every one of the Israelites before they started their journey. But when exactly was this done? And how, or by what?

The answers to these questions are found in the Books of the Chronicles of the kings of Israel. The biblical record shows that under the relatively short and wicked rule of King Ahaz, Israel slid deep into debauchery and idolatry. But when his son Hezekiah ascended to the throne, Israel enjoyed one of the greatest revivals in its long and colorful history. In the first year of King Hezekiah's reign, he repaired and sanctified the temple. Then he determined *"...to make a covenant with the Lord God of Israel, that His fierce wrath may turn away from us"* (2 Chronicles 29:10). This he accomplished by gathering the people and celebrating a special feast of Passover:

> *So they resolved to make a proclamation throughout all Israel, from Beersheba to Dan, that they should come to keep the Passover to the Lord God of Israel at Jerusalem, since they had not done it for a long time in the prescribed manner* (2 Chronicles 30:5).

> *For a multitude of the people...had not cleansed themselves, yet they ate the Passover contrary to what was written.* **But Hezekiah prayed for them**, *saying, "May the good Lord provide atonement for everyone who prepares his heart to seek God, the Lord God of his fathers, though he is not cleansed according to the purification of the sanctuary."* **And the Lord listened**

to Hezekiah and healed the people (2 Chronicles 30:18-20).

CONFIRMING THE COVENANT

One can see from these scriptures that the Passover feast did more than deliver Israel from slavery; it confirmed the Covenant and delivered them from sickness as well (see Exodus 15:26). Likewise, when we, as New Testament believers, partake of Communion properly and worthily, we affirm the New Covenant in Christ's blood, and *"by His stripes we are healed"* (see Luke 22:20; Isaiah 53:5).

This explains why the early church emphasized Communion as much as they did. Both Church history and the Book of Acts reveal that services at the time of the early church primarily centered around eating together and celebrating Communion (see Acts 2:42-47; 20:7). Breaking bread together confirms the Covenant horizontally, between brethren, and Communion confirms the Covenant vertically, between Christ and His Bride (see 1 Corinthians 10:16-17).

THE LAW OF JEALOUSY

But the story doesn't end there—there is bad news as well. As Paul warned the Corinthians, taking Communion unworthily can also be hazardous to one's health. When necessary, Communion brings chastisement! But what scripture did Paul get that revelation from? The answer lies buried deep within the "law of jealousy."

Speak to the children of Israel, and say to them: "If any man's wife goes astray and behaves unfaithfully toward him…if the spirit of jealousy comes upon him and he becomes jealous of his wife, who has defiled herself; or if the spirit of jealousy comes upon him and he becomes jealous of his wife, although she has not defiled herself—then the man shall bring his wife to the priest. He shall bring the offering required for her, one-tenth of an ephah of barley meal; he shall pour no oil on it and put no frankincense on it, because it is a grain offering of jealousy, an offering for remembering, for bringing iniquity to remembrance.

"The priest shall take holy water in an earthen vessel, **and take some of the dust that is on the floor of the tabernacle and put it into the water.**

"When he has made her drink the water, then it shall be, **if she has defiled herself and behaved unfaithfully toward her husband,** *that the water that brings a curse will enter her and become bitter, and* **her belly will swell, her thigh will rot,** *and the woman will become a curse among her people.* **But if the woman has not defiled herself, and is clean, then she shall be free and may conceive children** [Hebrew *seed*]. ***This is the law of jealousy…"*** (Numbers 5:12,14-15, 17, 27-29).

The only negative thing God ever said about Himself is, *"You shall worship no other god, for the Lord, whose name is Jealous, is a jealous God"* (Exodus 34:14). The Church is the Bride of Christ. When Christ's Bride is unfaithful and commits adultery, she is brought before the Priest—which in this case is Jesus, her jealous husband! There she is tried, and if found guilty, sentenced. But if she is innocent, *"…she shall be free* [from condemnation], *and shall conceive seed"* (Number 5:28 KJV). This judgment is accomplished every time a church (or an individual) takes Communion.

TWO TYPES OF CHASTISEMENT

When found guilty, her sentence will consist of one of two types of punishment. This is implicit in the statement, *"Her belly will swell, her thigh will rot."* One is spiritual (the belly represents one's spirit—see John 7:38 KJV); the other is natural (the thigh represents one's flesh—see Genesis 32:25 KJV). Each individual's chastisement is tailor-made for the occasion. The seed of the sin is always found in the fruit, and the fruit of sin is corruption. Spiritual sins birth unpleasant spiritual fruits, and the bitter consequences of natural sins are natural:

> *Do not be deceived, God is not mocked; for whatever a man sows, that he will also reap.* **For he who sows to his flesh will of the flesh reap corruption**, *but he who sows to the Spirit will of the Spirit reap everlasting life* (Galatians 6:7-8).

> *Therefore, having these promises, beloved, let us cleanse ourselves from all filthiness of the flesh and spirit, perfecting holiness in the fear of God* (2 Corinthians 7:1).

Spiritual chastisement is often accompanied by bouts of anger and emotional depression. It may also include alienation and separation from friends and family, sometimes even culminating in divorce. Natural chastisement, on the other hand, usually consists of things like sickness, financial troubles, debt, etc. When one's sin encompasses both the lust of the flesh and the pride of life (spiritual sin), the fruit is often a combination of both. Regardless of what type it is, *all* chastisement is unpleasant!

> *Now no chastening seems to be joyful for the present, but painful; nevertheless, afterward it yields the peaceable fruit of righteousness to those who have been trained by it* (Hebrews 12:11).

DUST—GOD'S REMINDER OF MERCY

One question always arises when this truth is first encountered—how and where does grace and mercy enter into this picture? The amazing answer is found in the dust of which we are made!

> *As a father pities his children, so the Lord pities those who fear Him. For He knows our frame; He remembers that we are dust* (Psalm 103:13-14).

When Moses gave the law of jealousy, he instructed the priest to put dust into the bitter water that the woman was made to drink. *"The priest shall take holy water in an earthen vessel, **and take some of the dust that is on the floor of the***

tabernacle and put it into the water" (Numbers 5:17). The law of jealousy is for the purpose of bringing iniquity to remembrance—*and the dust is God's reminder to be merciful!*

As the psalmist said:

He has not dealt with us according to our sins, nor punished us according to our iniquities (Psalm 103:10).

For He knows our frame; He remembers that we are dust (Psalm 103:14).

If You, Lord, should mark iniquities, O Lord, who could stand? (Psalm 130:3).

Although both God and the Law are impartial, God is merciful and the Law is not. The Law dealt only with the deeds and consequences of sin; God deals with the sinner. The Law meted out equal justice, but people aren't equal. Some people sin in defiance and rebellion, others in weakness and ignorance. Jesus said:

And that servant who knew his master's will, and did not prepare himself or do according to his will, shall be beaten with many stripes. But he who did not know, yet committed things deserving of stripes, shall be beaten with few… (Luke 12:47-48).

The wages of sin is death. Under the Law, all died in sin. Under grace, all who believe live in righteousness by the mercies of God and the Lamb. Amen!

Furthermore, we have had human fathers who corrected us, and we paid them respect. Shall we not much more readily be in subjection to the Father of spirits and live? (Hebrews 12:9)

QUESTIONS AND ANSWERS

1. If judgment comes through taking Communion, why should we take it? Wouldn't it be better simply to avoid it altogether?

No, because there is a double blessing in taking Communion. If we have sinned, it brings us to repentance. If our hearts are pure, it causes us to "conceive seed." (God's Word is His seed. Conceiving seed involves His promises coming to fruition in us. This includes the promises of healing!)

On the other hand, hardening our hearts and refusing to take Communion can bring devastating circumstances upon ourselves. Hebrews 3:12-14 admonishes us:

Beware, brethren, lest there be in any of you an evil heart of unbelief in departing from the living God; but exhort one another daily, while it is called "Today," lest any of you be hardened through the deceitfulness of sin. For we have become partakers of Christ if we hold the beginning of our confidence steadfast to the end.

It would be a serious mistake for a Christian to be conscious of the need for repentance and abstain from taking Communion instead of repenting. That would be choosing sin over righteousness. Instead of avoiding chastisement from God, it would invite Satan into the person's life for evil! It would not be a wise choice under any circumstances.

When given the opportunity to take Communion, the first thing we should each do is examine our conscience to make sure it is clear. We should also ask the Holy Spirit to bring anything to our remembrance that we should repent of, such as past or present offenses that we should forgive, etc. Paul said, *"But let a man examine himself, and so let him eat of the bread and drink of the cup"* (1 Corinthians 11:28).

2. Many people whose lifestyles are anything but righteous take Communion without any apparent negative consequences. Why aren't they chastised?

Because those who are serving Communion are simply following a tradition. Without the Spirit, it is nothing more than an empty ritual. They are not administering it in obedience to God's Word. The Passover element of Communion affords healing; the offering of jealousy aspect brings chastisement. Both are incorporated in Communion, but both features have to be taught and observed correctly before they are effective.

Notice the precise nature of the commandment in the text below—especially the part about the priest writing the curses in a book and scraping them into the bitter water. This corresponds to the minister who is serving Communion teaching the people *the full truth and consequences* of what they are doing before they actually partake of it:

> *...Then the priest shall put the woman under the oath of the curse, and he shall say to the woman—"the Lord make you a curse and an oath among your people, when the Lord makes your thigh rot and your belly swell; and*

may this water that causes the curse go into your stom-
ach, and make your belly swell and your thigh rot."
Then the woman shall say, "Amen, so be it." ***Then the***
priest shall write these curses in a book, and he
shall scrape them off into the bitter water. *And*
he shall make the woman drink the bitter water that
brings a curse, and the water that brings the curse shall
enter her to become bitter.

When he has made her drink the water, then it shall
be, if she has defiled herself and behaved unfaithfully
toward her husband, that the water that brings a curse
will enter her and become bitter, and her belly will
swell, her thigh will rot, and the woman will become
a curse among her people. ***But if the woman has not***
defiled herself, and is clean, then she shall be free
and may conceive children [Hebrew *seed*] (Numbers 5:21-24;27-28).

Paul teaches us that writing the curses in a book in the
Old Testament corresponds to writing them in the hearts of
believers in the New:

You are our epistle written in our hearts, known and
read by all men; clearly you are an epistle of Christ,
ministered by us, written not with ink but by the Spirit
of the living God, not on tablets of stone but on tablets
of flesh, that is, of the heart (2 Corinthians 3:2-3).

3. In the Bible, when Jesus initially introduced
Communion, the disciples ate a meal together
before it was observed. Is that the way it should

be done today? Is eating together an important, or even a necessary, part of Communion?

Yes, the very word *communion* means "an act of sharing" and is a translation of the Greek word *koinonia,* which means "partnership" or "participation."[1] Eating a communal meal is making and confirming covenant. We affirm our covenant with one another by "breaking bread" together, and we confirm our covenant with God through Christ by celebrating the bread and the wine in remembrance of Christ's death (see Matthew 26:26-28; Mark 14:22-24; 1 Corinthians 10:16; 11:26).

Biblical Communion was never meant to consist of a thimble of wine and a tiny cracker as it is commonly observed today. In Scripture, Communion was always celebrated after eating a communal meal, and it should continue to be observed that way today. In fact, the early church's custom was to eat together and have Communion every Sunday:

And [the early church] *continued steadfastly in the apostles' doctrine and fellowship,* **in the breaking of bread***, and in prayers* (Acts 2:42).

So continuing daily with one accord in the temple, **and breaking bread from house to house, they ate their food with gladness and simplicity of heart** (Acts 2:46).

Now on the first day of the week, **when the disciples came together to break bread***, Paul, ready to depart the next day, spoke to them and continued his message until midnight* (Acts 20:7).

Therefore, my brethren, when you come together to eat, wait for one another (1 Corinthians 11:33).

ENDNOTE

1. *Strong's Exhaustive Concordance*, Greek #2842.

Chapter Ten

UNANSWERED PRAYER

I awoke startled by the phone ringing loudly beside my bed. It was my brother. He was calling to ask me if I was interested in renting a house that someone told him about. What made his call so unusual was that it awakened me from a dream in which he had just asked me the exact same question! In the dream, I visited the house that he asked about and it was just what my wife and I were looking for. So when he called, I immediately told him yes, we were definitely interested.

When we actually went and looked at the house, it looked exactly as it had appeared in my dream! I was amazed—to say the least. We gave our present landlord two weeks notice and prepared to move. A few days later it started raining.

When the Saturday came around for us to move, it was still raining. My boss had graciously loaned me a large flat-bed trailer to move my furniture, but it was not covered. I drove out to the shop where I worked to pick up the trailer, silently praying as I went. I was thinking that when I got back to the house, I would call my brother to come over and help me pray for God to stop the rain. My thoughts were suddenly interrupted by a gentle, questioning voice, "Why are you going to wait?" Instantly, I knew God was asking me where *my* faith was. Why was I depending upon someone else's prayers? Although I was alone, I looked out the truck window and spoke out loud, "God is going to give us sunshine to move in!"

When I got back home with the trailer, I called my brother and asked him to come help me move. When he said something about moving in the rain, I assured him, "God is going to give us sunshine to move in." I am positive he didn't believe me, but God is faithful. By noon the rain had stopped and the clouds had rolled back to reveal bright blue skies. The sunshine lasted until we were bringing the last piece of furniture into the new house, at which time the raindrops began falling again. It rained for several more days before finally stopping.

THREE TYPES OF PRAYER

Answered prayer is a wonderful thing. However, the Bible reveals there are three distinct types of prayer—the prayer of *petition,* the prayer of *authority,* and the prayer of *appreciation*—and different circumstances demand different prayers. So how do we pick which one to use? Sometimes simply knowing which one is appropriate at a given time determines whether we receive what we are praying for or not.

We will examine each type individually. First, Jesus introduced petition prayer in the Gospel of Matthew. This particular prayer is commonly called the *Lord's prayer:*

In this manner, therefore, pray: Our Father in heaven, hallowed be Your name. Your kingdom come. Your will be done on earth as it is in heaven. Give us this day our daily bread. And forgive us our debts, as we forgive our debtors. And do not lead us into temptation, but deliver us from the evil one. For Yours is the kingdom and the power and the glory forever. Amen (Matthew 6:9-13).

Petition prayer, like all other types of prayer, is conditional. Jesus followed this model prayer with the following:

For if you forgive men their trespasses, your heavenly Father will also forgive you. But if you do not forgive men their trespasses, neither will your Father forgive your trespasses (Matthew 6:14-15).

HINDRANCES TO PRAYER

The obvious inference here is if we hold offense against someone in our hearts, God will not hear us when we pray. On the other hand, John said if we are obedient and our consciences are clear, we can be assured of receiving what we are asking for.

For if our heart condemns us, God is greater than our heart, and knows all things. Beloved, if our heart does not condemn us, we have confidence toward God. And whatever we ask we receive from Him, because we keep His commandments and do those things that are pleasing in His sight (1 John 3:20-22).

*Now this is the confidence that we have in Him, that if we ask anything according to His will, He hears us. And **if we know that He hears us**, whatever we ask, **we know that we have the petitions that we have asked of Him*** (1 John 5:14-15).

Obviously, it pays to forgive! In fact, achieving positive results through the prayer of authority is also dependent upon having a heart free from offense:

So Jesus answered and said to them, "Have faith in God. For assuredly, I say to you, whoever says to this mountain, 'Be removed and be cast into the sea,' and does not doubt in his heart, but believes that those things he says will be done, he will have whatever he says.

"And whenever you stand praying, if you have anything against anyone, forgive him, that your Father in heaven may also forgive you your trespasses. But if you do not forgive, neither will your Father in heaven forgive your trespasses" (Mark 11:22-23;25-26).

God is not even interested in receiving gifts from us, such as offerings of praise and prayers of thanksgiving, if we harbor offense in our hearts. He wants us to have a merciful heart toward those who have wronged us. Sometimes we even have to humble ourselves before those who hold grudges against us before we are pleasing in His sight:

Therefore if you bring your gift to the altar, and there remember that your brother has something against you, leave your gift there before the altar, and go...be reconciled to your brother, and then come and offer your gift (Matthew 5:23-24).

Although we cannot *make* people love us, it is necessary for us to do all that we can to keep peace. Paul said, *"If it is possible, as much as depends on you, live peaceably with all men"* (Romans 12:18). The answer to our prayers depends upon it!

Marital strife and division can also wreak havoc on our prayers, blocking them from ever getting off the ground. Peter admonished both husbands and wives to diligently set their houses in order to keep their prayers from being hindered:

> *Wives…be submissive to your own husbands, that even if some do not obey the word, they, without a word, may be won by the conduct of their wives.*

> *Husbands…dwell with them with understanding, giving honor to the wife, as to the weaker vessel, and as being heirs together of the grace of life, that your prayers may not be hindered* (1 Peter 3:1,7).

But even if we have hearts completely free from offense and have perfectly harmonious relationships with our spouses, it is still possible to ask in vain. As John said in First John 5:14, we must ask "according to His will" if we expect to receive what we are asking for. James reveals that the *motive* we have for asking for something is as important as *what* we are asking for. He said, *"You ask, and receive not, because you ask amiss, that you may consume it upon your lusts"* (James 4:3 KJV). Selfish prayers are seldom answered.

And finally, there is one last condition we must meet before God will receive our petitions. We must ask in humility. One of the best-known prayer admonitions in Scripture starts out with this condition:

If My people who are called by My name will humble themselves, and pray and seek My face, and turn from their wicked ways, then I will hear from heaven, and will forgive their sin and heal their land (2 Chronicles 7:14).

Humility is extra important because besides giving us the right attitude toward approaching the throne, it keeps us from asking with the wrong justification.

Also [Jesus] spoke this parable to some who trusted in themselves that they were righteous, and despised others: "Two men went up to the temple to pray, one a Pharisee and the other a tax collector. The Pharisee stood and prayed thus with himself, 'God, I thank You that I am not like other men—extortioners, unjust, adulterers, or even as this tax collector. I fast twice a week; I give tithes of all that I possess.' And the tax collector, standing afar off, would not so much as raise his eyes to heaven, but beat his breast, saying, 'God, be merciful to me a sinner!' I tell you, this man went down to his house justified rather than the other; for everyone who exalts himself will be humbled, and he who humbles himself will be exalted" (Luke 18:9-14).

Since humility is paramount to receiving what we are praying for, it is important to know how to go about the task of humbling ourselves. This is accomplished by simply being honest with ourselves. Self-righteousness is self-deception. *"For there is not a just man on earth who does good and does not sin"* (Ecclesiastes 7:20). No one else knows us like we know ourselves, so if we are honest we know that without

God's grace we are as weak and prone to sin as anyone else. That attitude leaves little room for pride.

A little fasting goes a long way toward enabling us to stay humble too. In fact, the Bible teaches that fasting helps with both humility *and* forgiveness. When David's own family and friends rewarded him "evil for good," he said, *"I humbled my soul with fasting"* (Psalm 35:12-13 KJV).

WHAT ABOUT FAITH?

You may be asking, "What about faith? You haven't mentioned faith as a condition for prayer being answered at all. Isn't faith a necessary ingredient too?" The answer may surprise you—it depends upon which kind of prayer you are praying! There are many prayers in Scripture that were answered even though the one praying was not in any condition to believe. A prime example is the desperate man who came to Jesus seeking healing for his dying son:

> *So Jesus came again to Cana of Galilee where He had made the water wine. And there was a certain noble-man whose son was sick at Capernaum. When he heard that Jesus had come out of Judea into Galilee, he went to Him and implored Him to come down and heal his son, for he was at the point of death.* **Then Jesus said to him, "Unless you people see signs and wonders, you will by no means believe."** *The nobleman said to Him, "Sir, come down before my child dies!" Jesus said to him, "Go your way; your son lives." So the man believed the word that Jesus spoke to him, and he went*

*his way. And as he was now going down, his servants met him and told him, saying, "Your son lives!" Then he inquired of them the hour when he got better. And they said to him, "Yesterday at the seventh hour the fever left him." So the father knew that it was at the same hour in which Jesus said to him, "Your son lives." **And he himself believed, and his whole household** (John 4:46-53).*

This man's petition was granted because of his desperation, not his faith. Jesus told him, in no uncertain terms, *"Unless you people see signs and wonders, you will by no means believe."* Jesus healed the boy so that the father *could* have faith, not *because of* his faith. It was not until the father confirmed the time of the boy's recovery that he became fully convinced that Jesus was the promised Messiah.

Gideon is another one God had to convince by showing signs and wonders before he could believe. Notice I said *could* believe, not *would* believe—there is a difference. Wanting to believe but not being able to is different from refusing to believe unless God shows you a sign. Wanting to but not being able to is doubt. Stubbornly refusing to believe unless God proves Himself to you is unbelief. Unbelief offends God; doubt challenges Him!

Unbelief is stubborn refusal to hear. It is clearly defined by Zechariah in his report of Judah's rebellion against God:

*But they refused to heed, shrugged their shoulders, and stopped their ears so that they could not hear. Yes, they made their hearts like flint, **refusing to hear** the law and the words which the Lord of hosts had sent by His*

Spirit through the former prophets. Thus great wrath came from the Lord of hosts (Zechariah 7:11-12).

Doubt, on the other hand, is a condition where one wants to believe but there is insufficient evidence to convince one's heart. Such was Gideon's case. When the angel approached him with God's plan for Israel's deliverance, his instant response revealed his heart:

> *And the Angel of the Lord appeared to him, and said to him, "The Lord is with you, you mighty man of valor!" Gideon said to Him, "O my lord, if the Lord is with us, why then has all this happened to us? **And where are all His miracles which our fathers told us about**, saying, 'Did not the Lord bring us up from Egypt?' But now the Lord has forsaken us and delivered us into the hands of the Midianites"* (Judges 6:12-13).

Gideon wanted to believe, and he knew about God's former exploits in delivering his forefathers from Egypt—yet Gideon had never seen a miracle with his own eyes. His desperate hunger to see his people delivered drew God's attention toward him, but now God had to convince him that he was the man for the job.

Gideon's *heart* had to be convinced, not just his head. Jesus said:

> *For assuredly, I say to you, whoever says to this mountain, "Be removed and be cast into the sea," **and does not doubt in his heart**, but believes that those things he says will be done, he will have whatever he says* (Mark 11:23).

Doubt hinders us from hearing God, and faith comes by hearing. Therefore God works to open our ears to hear and to let us know His will by performing miraculous signs and wonders for us to behold.

Jesus is the author and finisher of our faith (see Hebrews 12:2). Faith does not come from psyching ourselves up by reading the exploits of great men and women of faith, no matter how inspiring that may be. Nor, as some have taught, does faith come from memorizing and quoting Scripture. Genuine faith comes from hearing the living word that proceeds from the living God.

Miracles came easy for Peter and John because *"they had been with Jesus"* and had seen His power displayed many times (see Acts 4:13). So, although they had walked by the lame man at the gate of the temple every day for many days as they went to pray, when the day came for God to heal him, they heard Him clearly and did not hesitate to obey:

> *And a certain man lame from his mother's womb was carried,* **whom they laid daily at the gate of the temple** *which is called Beautiful, to ask alms of them that entered into the temple; who seeing Peter and John about to go into the temple asked an alms.*
>
> *And Peter, fastening his eyes upon him with John, said, Look on us. And he gave heed unto them, expecting to receive something of them. Then Peter said, Silver and gold have I none; but such as I have give I thee: in the name of Jesus Christ of Nazareth rise up and walk. And he took him by the right hand, and lifted him*

up: and immediately his feet and ankle bones received strength (Acts 3:2-7 KJV).

If Peter had tried that without hearing from God, he would have failed miserably. John said, *"...A man can receive nothing unless it has been given to him from heaven"* (John 3:27). That includes faith.

THE HEARING OF FAITH

Paul said that faith comes by hearing. We both receive and minister the Spirit by the *hearing* of faith:

> *This only I want to learn from you: Did you **receive the Spirit** by the works of the law, or **by the hearing of faith**?*

> *Therefore He who **supplies the Spirit** to you **and works miracles** among you, does He do it by the works of the law, or **by the hearing of faith**?* (Galatians 3:2,5)

Although at times we may *petition* God and still be heard even though our hearts are plagued with doubt, ministering effectively in the prayer of *authority* requires unwavering faith. Jesus said that a person can move a mountain if he *"does not doubt in his heart"* that it will move (see Mark 11:23). That level of faith only comes from hearing God. If we command a mountain to move without first hearing Him give the order, it will stubbornly resist all attempts to make it move.

So how do we get the mountain to obey? We petition God until we receive permission to give the command. In other words, petition prayer usually precedes the prayer of authority. For example, Jesus would often petition the Father at night, then minister using the prayer of authority during the day (see Mark 1:35,40-41; Luke 5:16,22-25).

Elijah is well known for defeating the prophets of Baal on Mount Carmel, but notice how he prayed right before the fire fell:

> *And it came to pass, at the time of the offering of the evening sacrifice, that Elijah the prophet came near and said, "Lord God of Abraham, Isaac, and Israel, let it be known this day that You are God in Israel and I am Your servant, and that **I have done all these things at Your word**"* (1 Kings 18:36).

When Elijah said, *"I have done all these things at **Your word**,"* he had to mean the God-breathed, inspired word (rhema), not the written Word (Logos), because there is nothing in the written Word telling him to do what he did. Likewise, shortly after his victory on Mount Carmel, Elijah petitioned God seven times *before* he warned Ahab to flee before the approaching rain (see 1 Kings 18:43-44).

AUTHORITY THROUGH COMMISSION

If one always has to hear God before operating in faith, how is it that certain ministers can seemingly minister at will—like certain prophets who regularly prophesy to everyone who is present? The answer is simple: the authority and ability to minister at will lies within one's *commission*.

When God commissions and sends someone to do a certain task, as when He sent Moses to deliver Israel from Egypt, He automatically gives that person sufficient authority to accomplish the task. He only has to give the order once. One command covers all (see Exodus 3:7-10; 6:13).

For example, in Matthew 10:1-8 Jesus gave the twelve apostles power over sickness, disease, and demons. Then He sent them to, *"Heal the sick, cleanse the lepers, raise the dead, [and] cast out demons…"* (Matthew 10:8). Once sent, they could minister accordingly. As Samuel told Saul when he anointed him king, *"And let it be…that you do as the occasion demands; for God is with you"* (1 Samuel 10:7). As long as we faithfully abide in Christ, act responsibly, and minister within the commission God has given us, we have full authority to do whatever is necessary to get the job done (see John 15:4,7).

Finally, just in case you've been wondering whether I really believe that it was my faith that stopped the rain that fateful Saturday when we were moving, the answer is a resounding *yes!* God has done far greater things than that!

Then Joshua spoke to the Lord in the day when the Lord delivered up the Amorites before the children of Israel, and he said in the sight of Israel: "Sun, stand still over Gibeon; and Moon, in the Valley of Aijalon." So the sun stood still, and the moon stopped, till the people had revenge upon their enemies. …So the sun stood still in the midst of heaven, and did not hasten to go down for about a whole day (Joshua 10:12-13).

Now that's a *real* miracle!

QUESTIONS AND ANSWERS

1. God knows everything. Since He knows our needs even before we ask, why do we have to pray?

Because of God's impartiality. God treats everyone equally, therefore if He does something for one person without someone justifying Him, He is then obligated to do the same thing for everyone else. Since He has about seven billion people to provide for, that would be a colossal error on His part, and He isn't known for making errors!

Prayer does not *persuade* God, it *justifies* God. He desires to do good things for His children, but it is a serious mistake to take His benevolence for granted. Without prayer or other forms of justification (fasting, sacrifice, service, obedience, etc.), even His elect will do without because God *"is no respecter of persons"* (Acts 10:34 KJV; also 2 Chronicles 7:14; Isaiah 1:18-19; 43:26; 1 John 3:22).

Being in covenant with God through Christ gives us access to the throne. It does not automatically give us what we want or need:

Let us therefore come boldly to the throne of grace, that we may obtain mercy and find grace to help in time of need (Hebrews 4:16).

2. Are there other conditions that we must meet before our prayers are answered besides the ones discussed in this chapter?

Yes, there are various and sundry conditions that must be met at one time or another. One is this: faith must always be accompanied by works (see James 2:26). For example, before Jesus would raise Lazarus from the dead, He required those present to remove the stone that was blocking the grave's entrance (see John 11:39-40). He could have easily commanded the stone to move and an angel would have rolled it out of the way—this is clearly revealed by the stone that was removed from His own grave at the time of His resurrection (see Matthew 28:2). But in the case of Lazarus, He instead required the people to move the stone.

When a strong man, fully armed, guards his own palace, his goods are in peace (Luke 11:21).

Chapter Eleven

TO BIND A STRONG MAN

I have made several mission trips to Africa, and on every trip I've encountered demonic manifestations similar to the ones recorded in the Bible. Demons have cried out of those possessed by them, or people have been violently thrown down and have writhed around on the floor. Of course, I've observed demonic activity while ministering here in the States too. It is just not quite as common.

Although I don't go looking for demons, when one manifests itself in a service there is not much else I can do but put a stop to the interruption. Usually that means casting it out. Ordinarily that is an easy task, but occasionally it is all but impossible. The disciples discovered this one day while Jesus was away.

And when [Jesus] *came to the disciples, He saw a great multitude around them…. Then one of the crowd… said, "Teacher, I brought You my son, who has a mute spirit. And wherever it seizes him, it throws him down; he foams at the mouth, gnashes his teeth, and becomes rigid. So I spoke to Your disciples, that they should cast it out, but they could not." He answered him and said,*

"O faithless generation, how long shall I be with you? How long shall I bear with you? Bring him to Me."

Then they brought him to Him. And when he saw Him, immediately the spirit convulsed him, and he fell on the ground and wallowed, foaming at the mouth. So He asked his father, **"How long has this been happening to him?"** *And he said,* **"From childhood.** *...But if You can do anything, have compassion on us and help us." Jesus said to him, "If you can believe, all things are possible to him who believes."* **Immediately the father of the child cried out and said with tears, "Lord, I believe; help my unbelief!"**

When Jesus saw that the people came running together, He rebuked the unclean spirit, saying to it, "Deaf and dumb spirit, I command you, come out of him **and enter him no more!"** *Then the spirit cried out, convulsed him greatly, and came out of him...* (Mark 9:14,17-26).

Why is deliverance easy one time and difficult another? The answer is in the keys. Jesus promised Peter that He was going to build His Church upon the revelation of who He was, and the gates of hell would not prevail against it (see Matthew 16:15-18). Then He said:

And I will give you **the keys** *of the kingdom of heaven, and whatever you bind on earth will be bound in heaven, and whatever you loose on earth will be loosed in heaven* (Matthew 16:19).

When the disciples tried to deliver the young boy who was born deaf, they attempted to use the promised authority to bind and loose, but they forgot the keys! They were just rattling the bars on the jailhouse door. Releasing someone from prison requires more than authority; it requires keys to open the prison cell. The judge has to authorize the prisoner's release, and the jailer has to either use the keys or turn them over to the one who is there to set the captive free.

Notice that Jesus dealt with the boy's father and drew a repentant confession of unbelief from him before commanding the demon to come out. Unbelief is sin! It is stubborn refusal to hear. The boy was deaf from birth. Because his forefathers *refused* to hear, the boy *couldn't* hear! The key to unlocking his jail cell was his father's repentance. Jesus first used the keys, then gave the command that loosed the boy and bound the devil:

> *Jesus…rebuked the unclean spirit, saying to it, "Deaf and dumb spirit, I command you, come out of him **and enter him no more!**" (Mark 9:25)*

This is the only place in Scripture where Jesus told a demon not to return. Why? Because it is the only recorded instance where He used the keys before He ministered deliverance. (Keys are knowledge—see Luke 11:52.) The rest of the time He informed the people the demons *would* return:

> *When an unclean spirit goes out of a man, he goes through dry places, seeking rest; and finding none, he says, "I will return to my house from which I came." And when he comes, he finds it swept and put in order. Then he goes and takes with him seven other spirits*

more wicked than himself, and they enter and dwell there; and the last state of that man is worse than the first (Luke 11:24-26).

Why did Jesus warn the Jews that the demons would return? Because they were willing to enjoy the fruit of His ministry but were unwilling to repent and obey His Word!

I BIND YOU SATAN!

Many ministers teach that you should bind a demon before casting it out by saying something like, "I bind you, devil"—but Jesus didn't. He never used the word *bind* at all. In fact, there is not a single instance in Scripture where anyone, including the apostles, ever told a demon that it was bound. Why? Because telling a devil that it is bound is like Delilah telling Samson that he was bound. It simply isn't effective.

How then does one bind demons? The same way Delilah finally bound Samson. She discovered his source of power and took it from him. Jesus said:

*When a strong man, fully armed, guards his own palace, his goods are in peace. But when a stronger than he comes upon him and overcomes him, **he takes from him all his armor in which he trusted**, and divides his spoils* (Luke 11:21-22).

Samson is the strong man of the Old Testament. His armor was his covenant (and the commission that he was given through that covenant). He was ordained to begin the process of delivering Israel from the Philistines even before he was conceived.

> *And the Angel of the Lord appeared to* [Samson's mother] *and said to her, "...Behold, you shall conceive and bear a son. And no razor shall come upon his head, for the child shall be a Nazirite to God from the womb;* ***and he shall begin to deliver Israel out of the hand of the Philistines"*** (Judges 13:3,5).

In the same way the deaf boy was *bound* from birth because of the sins of his forefathers, Samson was *free* from birth because of the covenant His mother made with God before he was born. Once Delilah discovered the terms of his covenant—one of which was that he was never to cut his hair—she had the battle won. When she cut his hair, his covenant was broken. Thus she took *"from him all his armor in which he trusted"* (see Luke 11:22).

Every covenant, along with the commission given through that covenant, is conditional. The disciples were commissioned to deliver the deaf boy through their covenant with God, but one of the conditions of their covenant was sincere *faith*. When they asked Jesus why they couldn't deliver him:

> *Jesus said to them, "Because of your unbelief; for assuredly, I say to you, if you have faith as a mustard seed, you will say to this mountain, 'Move from here to there,' and it will move; and nothing will be impossible for you"* (Matthew 17:20).

Every lock has a key. Every curse has a cause. The curse corresponds to the fruit, the cause to the root. The axe must be laid to the root of the tree or the tree will continue to bear fruit. When someone is bound, if you can find and deal with the source of the bondage, you have the victory in sight.

But what about *Christians* who are afflicted by demonic spirits? Can Christians who are filled with the Holy Spirit also have demons?

CAN CHRISTIANS HAVE DEMONS?

The answer is *yes, they not only can, many do!* Paul addresses this problem in his second letter to the Corinthian church:

> But I fear, lest somehow, as the serpent deceived Eve by his craftiness, so your minds may be corrupted from the simplicity that is in Christ. For if he who comes preaches another Jesus whom we have not preached, **or if you receive a different spirit which you have not received**, or a different gospel which you have not accepted—you may well put up with it! (2 Corinthians 11:3-4)

Why would Paul fear something that cannot happen? The Corinthians were Christians, yet Paul feared they might receive another spirit in addition to the Holy Spirit (which, considering his concern, meant he feared they might receive an evil spirit!). His concern was well-founded, and it reveals a very real problem that today's church has largely ignored—or worse, has even denied that it exists.

The most common objection used against this truth stems from the belief that God will not dwell in a person who has an evil spirit. The problem with this belief is it ignores both Scripture and reality! God is the One who cleans the house.

He usually takes out the rubbish after He buys the house, not before. Sanctification takes place after salvation, as Israel's first two feasts clearly illustrate. *All leaven* is removed from the house starting the day *after* Passover, and this continues for a total of seven days (see Leviticus 23:5-6). *Seven* means "all" or "complete."

God dwells in His people's hearts, united with their spirits. Demons dwell in the flesh and work through the *"desires of the flesh and of the* [carnal] *mind"* (Ephesians 2:3). This is similar to a tenant living in a house with termites in the walls. The tenant works to maintain the house, but the termites work secretly to destroy it. This simple analogy explains why so many Christians suffer from demonic oppressions such as emotional depression, anger, anxieties, inordinate sexual lusts, and the like.

Termites love darkness because they cannot abide sunlight. Demons love darkness as well. Paul was explicit in exposing their presence. He said:

> *For we wrestle not against flesh and blood, but against principalities, against powers, against the rulers of the darkness of this world, against spiritual wickedness in high places* (Ephesians 6:12 KJV).

As long as we are ignorant of Satan's tactics, he has the upper hand.

The consequences of this error have been disastrous to the Church. The devil has had a heyday. Satan himself has convinced the saints that he can be bound simply by them telling him that he is. Christians have bought into the lie that they cannot possibly have demons, therefore they never go for deliverance. When they do go to their ministers for help, they are told there is nothing that can be done for them because the problems they are contending with are in reality just their flesh.

The thief has stole the truth, killed the effectiveness of the Word, and destroyed many of God's children, while at the same time convincing the Church that he hardly even exists. God said, *"My people are destroyed for lack of knowledge..."* (Hosea 4:6).

Nothing proves God's supremacy over His creation more than His power over Satan. Jesus said, *"But if I cast out demons by the Spirit of God, surely the kingdom of God has come upon you"* (Matthew 12:28). He also told us to cast them out. It is about time we took on the task!

QUESTIONS AND ANSWERS

1. In Galatians 3:13, Paul said that Christ has redeemed us from the curse of the Law. How can a Christian be under a curse if Christ has redeemed us from the curse?

Indeed, Christians are free from the curses of the Law of *Moses,* but his Law isn't the only source of curses. For example, many curses are self-inflicted through the eternal law of reciprocity:

*While the earth remains, **seedtime and harvest**, cold and heat, winter and summer, and day and night **shall not cease*** (Genesis 8:22).

Do not be deceived, God is not mocked; for whatever a man sows, that he will also reap. For he who sows to his flesh will of the flesh reap corruption, but he who sows to the Spirit will of the Spirit reap everlasting life (Galatians 6:7-8).

The law of reciprocity reveals why Jesus warned us not to judge one another. When we judge (make a formula concerning someone), whether good or bad, we are placed under the formula we make.

Another source of curses is breaking the ever-present "royal law," which will never pass away: *"If you fulfill the royal law according to the scripture, Thou shalt love thy neighbor as thyself, you do well"* (James 2:8 KJV).

The law of reciprocity and the royal law are based upon the principles of righteousness contained within the Law of Moses. These principles are eternal. Jesus said they would never pass away until "all is fulfilled" (see Matthew 5:18). Christ's cross dealt only with the "carnal ordinances" of the Law, which the writer of Hebrews said were *"imposed until the time of reformation"* (Hebrews 9:10). Paul also taught the same thing—that the cross wiped out the Law's ordinances but not its righteous principles:

Blotting out the handwriting of ordinances that was against us, which was contrary to us, and took it out of the way, nailing it to his cross (Colossians 2:14 KJV).

For we know that the law is spiritual, but I am carnal, sold under sin (Romans 7:14).

The fact that certain types of curses are still present and prevalent even after Christ shed His blood on the cross is shown by John's use of the future tense in Revelation 22:3 (notice he said, *"There **shall be** no more curse,"* not "there *is* no more curse"):

> ***And there shall be no more curse***, *but the throne of God and of the Lamb shall be in it, and His servants shall serve Him.*

Once Jesus returns and resurrects the saints and gives them new bodies, as John said, there will truly be "no more curse." Until then, there are many who are afflicted by various curses, and they need help through biblical counseling and deliverance!

2. Do all Christians have the authority to cast out demons or only certain ones?

It is generally conceded that all "believers" have a limited amount of authority over demons. This is based on Mark 16:17, where Jesus said, *"These signs will follow those who believe: In My name they will cast out demons...."* In reality, when God's people were in bondage to their enemies in the Old Testament, He raised up anointed "deliverers" to set them free. Similarly, He raises up anointed ministers to deliver His people today.

Jesus said casting out demons is a work of miracles, and Paul asked, *"Are all workers of miracles?"* implying that everyone is not (see 1 Corinthians 12:29). God gives specific people a special anointing and commission to cast out demons.

Now John answered Him, saying, "Teacher, we saw someone who does not follow us casting out demons in Your name, and we forbade him because he does not follow us." But Jesus said, "Do not forbid him, for no one who works a miracle in My name can soon afterward speak evil of Me" (Mark 9:38-39).

3. What does the Bible mean when it says, *"No one can enter a strong man's house and plunder his goods, unless he first binds the strong man"*? (Mark 3:27.) What is a strong man, and how does one actually go about binding one?

First, it is important to know that all demons are not "strong men." Only a demon who is justified in seizing and holding someone in bondage because of the person's sin (or the sin of the person's forefathers, as the case may be) is a legitimate, biblical "strong man."

As we previously discussed, Jesus gave us a perfect example in Mark 9:23-25 of how to bind such demons by effectively and efficiently removing their authority when he led the deaf boy's father to repent and confess his sin. Following Jesus's example, we can see that before we can cast out a strong man (which in effect binds it), we must remove the root justification for its occupation. This is done by locating the specific sin or sins that gave it a legal claim to his victim. The victim must repent and confess his or her sin (and when necessary renounce the hidden things of darkness—see 2 Corinthians 4:2). Sometimes restitution is also required:

If the wicked restores the pledge, gives back what he has stolen, and walks in the statutes of life without committing iniquity, he shall surely live; he shall not die (Ezekiel 33:15).

Once this is accomplished, the demon(s) should be commanded to come out and to release its hold on the person and his or her goods (emotional, mental, and physical health; finances; etc.). Prayers for restoration (prosperity, healing, etc.) should follow the exorcism.

An example of what the Bible means when it speaks of demons being bound is found in Second Peter 2:4:

For if God did not spare the angels who sinned, but cast them down to hell and delivered them into chains of darkness, to be reserved for judgment.

Here Peter says that the angels who sinned—now known as demons—were bound by "chains of darkness." These demons are bound only in the sense that they cannot return to their first estate. They have chosen darkness and cannot repent and revert back to light. Similarly, when Jesus cast the demon out of the young boy who was deaf, He bound the demon by commanding it to leave and forbidding it to return. As we have previously stated, He had the authority to do so because the boy's father repented.

RECOMMENDED READING

The Anatomy of a Scorpion by Ira L. Milligan. Jesus said, "*Behold, I give unto you power to tread on serpents and scorpions, and over all the power of the enemy…*" (Luke 10:19 KJV). This book reveals the truth and power in the symbolism of the scorpion and gives practical application for every believer. It includes instructions and procedures to use in dealing with demonic spirits and is a must for anyone interested in counseling and deliverance.

Chapter Twelve

THE BELIEVER'S PRIESTHOOD

Ioften wonder how certain heresies get started. Sometimes their origins can be traced to specific persons, but some seem to defy all attempts at locating their sources. Heresy is an insidious parasite, thriving by feeding upon truth. Like counterfeit money, it cannot exist alone. It has to have the substance of truth to survive. So regardless of how difficult it is to locate the original creator of a given heresy, it is relatively easy to find the scriptural justification for its existence.

Such is the case with the often-quoted but never substantiated doctrine that declares, "The husband is the priest of the home." Without question, the scriptural sources of this heresy are First Peter 2:5 and Ephesians 5:23:

You also, as living stones, are being built up a spiritual house, a holy priesthood, to offer up spiritual sacrifices acceptable to God through Jesus Christ (1 Peter 2:5).

For the husband is head of the wife, as also Christ is head of the church; and He is the Savior of the body (Ephesians 5:23).

If you are one of those who have received and believed this heresy without first examining it closely, you are probably asking, "What do you mean *heresy?* If the husband is the head of the wife, doesn't that automatically make him the priest of his home?"

My answer is this: If it does, then where does that leave her if he is lost, or even worse, if he is a Satanist? Is she automatically condemned to hell with him? That is not the only thing wrong with this teaching. It also negates or diminishes the wife's priesthood, making it subordinate to her husband's. The home has only one "High Priest"—His name is *Jesus!* As in the Levitical priesthood of Israel, all other priests are equal.

Those who teach this doctrine are obviously motivated by the desire for men to step up to the plate and accept their proper leadership roles in their homes; nevertheless, the consequences of this doctrine, like all heresy, can be dangerous. It has the potential of backfiring and giving men authority over their wives that God never meant for them to wield.

AUTHORITY AND RESPONSIBILITY

All authority is from God. He never gives authority without corresponding responsibility. Husbands are not responsible for their wives' salvation. Therefore they have no authority to tell them how or whom to worship (which they would have if they assume the role of high priest in their homes). Otherwise, men who are Satanists, which regrettably some are, would inadvertently bring eternal damnation upon their wives and children. Instead, Paul said the following regarding cases like these:

> *The unbelieving husband is sanctified by the wife, and the unbelieving wife is sanctified by the husband; otherwise your children would be unclean, but now they are holy* (1 Corinthians 7:14).

Salvation is an individual, personal responsibility. A wife is not responsible for her husband's salvation, nor is he responsible for hers. His authority is limited by his duties as a husband. He should be the shepherd of his home, lovingly tending his family as a shepherd tends his flock, but this does not make him its priest.

What then is meant by the *priesthood* of the believer? What does it entail to be a priest? Peter condensed it into one sentence in the scripture quoted above—a priest is authorized *"...to offer up spiritual sacrifices acceptable to God through Jesus Christ"* (1 Peter 2:5). Among other things, our priesthood is what enables us to *"...come boldly to the throne of grace, that we may obtain mercy and find grace to help in time of need"* (Hebrews 4:16). It also authorizes us to make intercession for others. Without it, we would have to use an earthly mediator instead of the heavenly One that we now have (*"For there is one God and **one Mediator** between God and men, the Man Christ Jesus"*—1 Timothy 2:5).

Under the Levitical priesthood, only Aaron and his descendants were allowed to offer up sacrifices to God. All others were severely censored when they attempted to do so. A prime example is King Uzziah:

But when [King Uzziah] was strong his heart was lifted up, to his destruction, for he transgressed against the Lord his God by entering the temple of the Lord to burn incense on the altar of incense. So Azariah the priest went in after him, and with him were eighty priests of the Lord—valiant men. And they withstood King Uzziah, and said to him, "It is not for you, Uzziah, to burn incense to the Lord, but for the priests, the sons of Aaron, who are consecrated to burn incense. Get out of the sanctuary, for you have trespassed! You shall have no honor from the Lord God." Then Uzziah became furious; and he had a censer in his hand to burn incense. And while he was angry with the priests, leprosy broke out on his forehead, before the priests in the house of the Lord, beside the incense altar. And Azariah the chief priest and all the priests looked at him, and there, on his forehead, he was leprous; so they thrust him out of that place. Indeed he also hurried to get out, because the Lord had struck him (2 Chronicles 26:16-20).

It was a very serious mistake to come into God's presence without being a priest. Even Levites who were not priests (those who were uncles and cousins but not sons of Aaron) were forbidden to burn incense. Korah made this mistake. Although the passage is too long to quote in its entirety, excerpts are quoted below:

Now Korah…rose up before Moses with some of the children of Israel, two hundred and fifty leaders of the congregation…. They gathered together against Moses and Aaron, and said to them, "You take too much upon yourselves, for all the congregation is holy, every one of them, and the Lord is among them. Why then do you exalt yourselves above the assembly of the Lord?"

So when Moses heard it, he fell on his face; and he spoke to Korah and all his company, saying, "Tomorrow morning the Lord will show who is His and who is holy.... Do this: Take censers...put fire in them and put incense in them before the Lord tomorrow, and it shall be that the man whom the Lord chooses is the holy one...."

Then Moses said to Korah, "Hear now, you sons of Levi: Is it a small thing to you that the God of Israel has separated you from the congregation of Israel...to do the work of the tabernacle of the Lord, and to stand before the congregation to serve them; and that He has brought you near to Himself, you and all your brethren, the sons of Levi, with you? And are you seeking the priesthood also?"

So every man took his censer, put fire in it, laid incense on it....

And Moses said: "By this you shall know that the Lord has sent me to do all these works, for I have not done them of my own will. If these men die naturally like all men...then the Lord has not sent me. But if the Lord creates a new thing, and the earth opens its mouth and swallows them up with all that belongs to them, and they go down alive into the pit, then you will understand that these men have rejected the Lord."

Now it came to pass…that the ground split apart under them, and the earth opened its mouth and swallowed them up, with their households and all the men with Korah, with all their goods. So they and all those with them went down alive into the pit; the earth closed over them, and they perished from among the assembly (Numbers 16:1-10;18;28-33).

Not only does our priesthood open the door for our prayers and intercessions, as these scriptures show, it makes our bodies and members acceptable as well:

I beseech you therefore, brethren, by the mercies of God, that you present your bodies a living sacrifice, holy, acceptable to God, which is your reasonable service (Romans 12:1).

NEITHER MALE NOR FEMALE

The opposite extreme to making the husband the *spiritual* head of the home is when Galatians 3:28 is used to negate all differences between the sexes, both in the home and in ministry: *"There is neither Jew nor Greek, there is neither slave nor free, there is neither male nor female; for you are all one in Christ Jesus."*

Both errors originate from the same source—taking scriptures out of their context and not rightly dividing the Word of truth. A husband is the *natural* head of his home, and as such, he has specific natural authority and responsibilities. In *spiritual* matters, both the husband and wife have equal access to God's throne—thus their roles as priests before God are equal as well.

This equality does not erase or annul the requirements and limitations that God Himself has placed upon people in their service to Him or in their natural roles as husbands and wives. To please God, wives must walk in obedience to their own husbands and husbands must love their wives:

> *Therefore, just as the church is subject to Christ, so let the wives be to their own husbands in everything. Husbands, love your wives, just as Christ also loved the church and gave Himself for her* (Ephesians 5:24-25).

As for spiritual matters in the home, both husbands and wives have similar duties. The following admonition was given to all Israel, not just to the men:

> *Hear, O Israel.... You shall love the Lord your God with all your heart, with all your soul, and with all your strength. And these words which I command you today shall be in your heart.* **You shall teach them diligently to your children, and shall talk of them when you sit in your house,** *when you walk by the way, when you lie down, and when you rise up* (Deuteronomy 6:4-7).

All authority is of God. There are two divisions (natural and spiritual) and seven levels of authority. When one level of authority conflicts with another, the Bible commands us to obey the "higher power" (see Romans 13:1 KJV; also Acts 5:29).

SEVEN LEVELS OF AUTHORITY

The first level of authority is God the Father. The second is the Spirit of Truth; the third is the written Word of God. Next is conscience. After that comes civil authority, followed by the authority of fathers and husbands. And the last, and least, level includes the natural authority mothers have over their children, the natural authority employers exercise over their employees, and the limited natural and spiritual authority pastors have over their flocks.

Both wives and children are to obey their respective authorities "in the Lord," meaning they are not to obey when given commands contrary to the will and Word of God (see Colossians 3:18; Ephesians 6:1). For example, a man cannot require his wife to accompany him in an act that is against the law, nor can he require her to do something that would defile her conscience.

In cases where the wife works a public job, the husband's authority overrides the authority of his wife's employer, otherwise the wife would have two "heads." A wife's ultimate loyalty and obedience should always be to her husband, not to her employer. Similarly, married women who minister publically should carefully balance their natural obligations to obey and serve their husbands with their spiritual obligations to fulfill their ministries (see 1 Corinthians 7:3-5).

When husbands assume spiritual authority over their wives or wives assume natural authority over their husbands, they err. Likewise, pastors have to be very careful not to assume natural authority over other men's wives and to stay well within the boundaries of both the natural and spiritual authority that is awarded them by their offices. No person's authority goes beyond that for which he or she is responsible.

Natural and spiritual authority must be delicately balanced, regardless of where and in what manner it is used. There are times when natural authority overrides spiritual (which is the norm), and at other times spiritual authority takes precedence over the natural. Either way, truth is always balanced. To please God, authority must be exercised properly without partiality or selfishness. Invariably, selfishness leads to abuse, and abuse leads to extremes. May God help us all.

> *The God of Israel said, the Rock of Israel spoke to me: "He who rules over men must be just, ruling in the fear of God"* (2 Samuel 23:3).

QUESTIONS AND ANSWERS

1. What is meant by natural and spiritual authority? What is the difference between the two?

Natural authority concerns natural things, such as family discipline, education, secular careers, money, health, sexual relations between husband and wives, recreation, and the like. Spiritual authority deals with such things as righteousness, preaching, prophesying, worship, morality, integrity, and honesty. One has to do with natural responsibilities and the other has to do with spiritual. Sometimes they overlap. For example, the husband is responsible to provide for his family, so his pastor should not tell him when and where he should work. But if he goes to work in a bar where nudity is the norm, then the case enters into the spiritual realm. He would then be living in unrighteousness and immorality. In that case the pastor can forbid him from working there or excommunicate him if he refuses to quit.

2. Are there times when natural authority overrides spiritual authority?

Yes, in fact, when conflict arises on the same level, the norm is *natural authority takes precedence over spiritual.* This rule is the basis for Paul's admonition in First Corinthians 14:32, *"And the spirits of the prophets are subject to the prophets."* Another example is a woman's spiritual ministry is subject to her father's authority if she is still living at home, or to her husband's if she is married. This principle is established in the law of vows:

> *Or if a woman makes a vow to the Lord, and binds herself by some agreement while in her father's house in her youth, and her father hears her vow and the agreement by which she has bound herself, and her father holds his peace, then all her vows shall stand, and every agreement with which she has bound herself shall stand. But if her father overrules her on the day that he hears, then none of her vows nor her agreements by which she has bound herself shall stand; and the Lord will release her, because her father overruled her.*
>
> *If indeed she takes a husband, while bound by her vows or by a rash utterance from her lips by which she*

bound herself, and her husband hears it, and makes no response to her on the day that he hears, then her vows shall stand, and her agreements by which she bound herself shall stand. But if her husband overrules her on the day that he hears it, he shall make void her vow which she took and what she uttered with her lips, by which she bound herself, and the Lord will release her (Numbers 30:3-8).

In Scripture kings ruled over prophets (though sometimes to their own hurt!—see 2 Chronicles 25:16). Likewise, prophets should submit to the pastors of the churches where they minister. Another example is the rule governing slaves. Paul said that a slave is the Lord's freedman, meaning that because he (or she) is a slave, God does not require anything of him other than that he must diligently and faithfully serve his master:

For he who is called in the Lord while a slave is the Lord's freedman. Likewise he who is called while free is Christ's slave (1 Corinthians 7:22).

Our priorities should be God first, family second, ministry third. God requires men to provide for their families, so unless He calls the husband into full-time ministry and puts him on His own payroll, family obligations take precedence over his ministry:

But if anyone does not provide for his own, and especially for those of his household, he has denied the faith and is worse than an unbeliever (1 Timothy 5:8).

3. You said the husband should shepherd his family. What is the difference between a husband being the priest of his home and being the shepherd?

There is a significant difference between the two. Priesthood relates to the vertical relationship between God and man, and shepherding pertains to the horizontal relationship between brethren. Priesthood refers specifically to God's acceptance of our prayers and spiritual sacrifices. Through Christ, God accepts all believers equally, for *"there is neither Jew nor Greek, there is neither slave nor free, there is neither male nor female; for you are all one in Christ Jesus"* (Galatians 3:28). This gives all God's children equal rights to come into His presence *"...to offer up spiritual sacrifices acceptable to God through Jesus Christ"* (1 Peter 2:5).

The horizontal aspect of shepherding and the natural authority that is inherent in its administration are the primary reasons the Bible places some minor restrictions and limitations upon a woman's ministry (see 1 Timothy 2:12-14).

4. Is there ever a time when the wife (or mother) becomes the legitimate spiritual leader of her home?

Yes, if the husband is a nonbeliever, the believing wife automatically becomes the spiritual leader. As such, she is responsible to diligently teach the Word of God to her children (see Deuteronomy 6:7). The same thing is true if she is a single parent (widow, divorcée, etc.). Also, if the husband is an unbeliever, between the two of them she is the only one with a legitimate priesthood (see John 9:31).

Her responsibility to shepherd her children does not extend to her unbelieving husband. Although she should pray for his salvation, she is to avoid offending him with the Word or by trying to be his "Holy Spirit," convincing and convicting him of his sin. In this type of situation, Peter's admonition to wives with lost or lukewarm husbands comes into play:

> *Wives...be submissive to your own husbands, that even if some do not obey the word, they, without a word, may be won by the conduct of their wives* (1 Peter 3:1).

Her conduct and lifestyle should say it all!

RECOMMENDED READING

Euroclydon by Ira L. Milligan. *Euroclydon* defines and illustrates the four winds of heaven as they oppose the four winds of the earth (see Daniel 7:2; Revelation 7:1). As this ancient conflict unfolds, the role of the prophetic and apostolic ministries in the end-time church is revealed. *Euroclydon* reveals several changes necessary before these ministries can be fully restored.

Chapter Thirteen

CUTTING CORNERS

Of all the mysteries contained in the Law of Moses, none intrigue me more than *the law of cutting corners*:

When you reap the harvest of your land, **you shall not wholly reap the corners of your field**, *nor shall you gather the gleanings of your harvest. And you shall not glean your vineyard, nor shall you gather every grape of your vineyard; you shall leave them for the poor and the stranger: I am the Lord your God* (Leviticus 19:9-10).

The obvious inference here is God wanted the produce grown in the corners of the fields and the gleaning of the vineyards left for *"the poor and the stranger"* in the land. Another way of saying this is , as the Israelites reaped their fields they were to "round off" the corners, and in so doing give grace to those who were less fortunate than they were. Conversely, the law concerning trimming beards has the opposite meaning:

You shall not shave around the sides of your head, nor shall you disfigure the edges [corners] *of your beard* (Leviticus 19:27).

They were commanded to round off the corners of their fields, thus giving grace to the poor and stranger, but when it came to the corners of their beards, they were required to do the opposite. They were forbidden to round them off! What is the hidden message in the parable contained in this second law? It is this: God wants us to give grace to others while at the same time holding ourselves to a standard higher than we require of them.

There is no command in the Law more important than this one when it comes to understanding and teaching doctrinal truth. Knowing the truth doesn't give us the right to despise and ridicule those who are less fortunate than us. Jesus told the self-righteous Pharisees to *"go and learn what this means: 'I desire mercy and not sacrifice'…"* (Matthew 9:13). Then later He reproved them, *"But if you had known what this means, 'I desire mercy and not sacrifice,' you would not have condemned the guiltless"* (Matthew 12:7).

Grace is merciful. Grace seeks to excuse instead of accuse. It is a grievous error to despise someone for not knowing the truth. As often as not, a person is ignorant because his or her religious leaders have not taught him what he really needs to know. Another thing that should always be taken into consideration when judging others is what John the Baptist said in John 3:27: *"…A man can receive nothing unless it has been given to him from heaven."* Regardless of how *we* judge people, God holds them accountable only if *He* has shown them the truth. Jesus said:

> *If I had not come and spoken to them, they would have no sin, but now they have no excuse for their sin.*

If I had not done among them the works which no one else did, they would have no sin; but now they have seen and also hated both Me and My Father (John 15:22,24).

God is gracious. He only reveals truth to His elect as they are able to receive it, not before. Jesus told His disciples, *"I still have many things to say to you, but you cannot bear them now"* (John 16:12). Only He knows when we can bear more truth. To require people to receive truth prematurely is both futile and foolhardy.

When Jesus was traveling to Jerusalem to be lifted up, He encountered opposition from some Samaritans when He attempted to enter their village. James and John reacted by asking permission to call fire down from heaven upon them the way Elijah did. Instead of giving them permission, Jesus rebuked them! He said, *"You do not know what manner of spirit you are of. For the Son of Man did not come to destroy men's lives but to save them"* (Luke 9:55-56).

A few short years later Philip went to the same area where the Truth (Jesus) was previously rejected and *"preached Christ to them"* (see Acts 8:5-8). The same people who previously had hardened their hearts against Christ now received Him with open arms—and a great spiritual revival broke out!

When we walk in self-righteous pride instead of true holiness, allowing knowledge to "puff us up," we are walking in dangerous territory (see 1 Corinthians 8:1). This judgmental attitude is highly offensive to God.

I have spread out my hands all the day unto a rebellious people, which walk in a way that was not good, after *their own thoughts…which say, Stand by thyself, come not near to me; **for I am holier than thou**. These are a smoke in my nose, a fire that burns all the day* (Isaiah 65:2,5 KJV).

Knowing the truth doesn't make one person holier than another. In fact, it does not make one holy at all. Living and walking in the truth produces holiness (see Romans 6:13,22). As the law of cutting corners reveals, those who walk in true holiness and righteousness humbly and graciously extend mercy to those who are less fortunate than they are.

THE PRIMARY PURPOSE OF HERESY

The primary purpose of heresy is to conceal truth. If we think we already understand something, we will not continue searching for the truth. Therefore, Satan's tactic is to hand us half-truths and deceptions, which, though they have little or no real value, nevertheless are effective in keeping us from searching for the precious treasures hidden in the Word.

Jesus said that God has *"hidden these things from the wise and prudent and revealed them to babes"* (Luke 10:21). One psalmist exclaimed to the Lord, *"Open thou mine eyes, that I may behold wondrous things out of thy law"* (Psalm 119:18 KJV). As the law of cutting corners reveals, God has hidden many spiritual treasures by putting them in plain sight but disguising them as natural ordinances and laws.

Conversely, the primary way Satan hides truth is through false revelation. Every worthless deception covers a precious treasure. By removing the deceptive covering, we reveal the shining jewel hidden beneath.

FALLEN ANGELS

An example of this is the ancient adage that states, "God has two-thirds of the angels and Satan has one-third." It sounds encouraging because there are more with us than with the devil, but is it true? Also, where did it come from? What scripture is it based upon?

There is only one scripture that this statement could have originated from. Although in Luke 10:18 Jesus said that He saw Satan fall from heaven, and Peter talks about angels being "cast down" in Second Peter 2:4, neither Jesus nor Peter mentioned how *many* there were that fell. In the entire Bible only Revelation 12:3-4 *appears* to talk about a third of the angels falling:

> *And another sign appeared in heaven: behold, a great, fiery red dragon having seven heads and ten horns…. His tail drew a third of the stars of heaven and threw them to the earth….*

The first hurdle we have to overcome before we can safely assume this scripture actually describes falling angels is this: how can Revelation 12:3-4 be referring to something that happened at least four thousand years before it was written— in fact, all the way back to the third chapter of Genesis? The Book of Revelation begins, *"The Revelation of Jesus Christ, which God gave unto him, to show unto his servants things which must shortly come to pass…"* (Revelation 1:1 KJV).

Revelation is all about the future—that is, the future from John's perspective. John saw *"things which must shortly come to pass,"* not events that took place thousands of years before he was born!

Another important question that needs to be answered is, since this adage declares that God has one-third more support than Satan, why would the devil propagate a lie that gives God the edge in their warfare? There is only one logical reason: to hide something that is even more damaging to his cause—the truth!

The truth is Revelation 12:3-4 is not talking about angels falling at all; it is talking about *saints* falling! Throughout Scripture the primary meaning of *stars* is people, not angels. For example, in Genesis 15:5 God told Abraham, *"...'Look now toward heaven, and count the stars if you are able to number them.' And He said to him, 'So shall your descendants be.'"* Likewise, the Lord told Daniel that in the resurrection, *"Those who are wise shall shine like the brightness of the firmament, and those who turn many to righteousness like the stars forever and ever"* (Daniel 12:3).

The reason the devil introduced this *seemingly* harmless heresy is because John exposed Satan's bloody end-time plans in Revelation 12:3-4. This is one of the clearest passages in the Bible warning the Church of what will happen immediately before Christ returns. It reveals there will be major worldwide persecution. The Church is destined for a virtual bloodbath. Joel prophesied that in the last days the moon, which is a symbol for the Church, will be turned into blood (see Joel 2:31).

How severe will this persecution be? *Very severe!* One-third of the Church will be brought down by the tail of the dragon (the dragon's tail is the false prophet of Revelation 19:20—see also Isaiah 9:15; Daniel 11:33-35).

GETTING READY

Previously, in Chapter Two, I briefly introduced the fast-approaching, end-time persecution of the Church. I bring it up once again to emphasize the importance and necessity of being prepared for it. The Church is in major transition at the present time, and one of the primary reasons for the change is God is preparing us for what lies ahead.

Paul fervently warned the world that perilous times were coming, especially toward the end of the age. He prophesied of fierce, ungodly people who would be very *religious,* yet despisers of the righteous (see 2 Timothy 3:1-4). Similarly, Jesus said the time was coming when people would kill His followers and think they were doing God a favor (see John 16:2).

The recent, worldwide threat imposed by Islamic extremists and their suicidal attacks upon innocent people amply authenticates both Paul's and Christ's prophetic warnings. In the name of their god these religious fanatics brutally behead people who have done nothing more than be in the wrong place at the wrong time—especially if they are Christians. Persecution is now a present-tense reality. As the socialists and communists of the twentieth century learned, and history confirms, there is only one type of church that can survive the vicious onslaught that is rising up and challenging us today—*the underground church.*

Those who choose to blithely ignore the prophetic revelation that God is pouring out upon the Church in this hour are destined for a rude awakening. Although John received his vision of impending persecution two thousand years ago, it is *"for an appointed time, but at the end it shall speak…wait for it; because it will surely come, it will not tarry"* (Habakkuk 2:3 KJV). Jesus is coming soon. It is time for His Bride to wash and iron her wedding gown and prepare herself for His return.

> *And behold, I am coming quickly, and My reward is with Me, to give to every one according to his work* (Revelation 22:12).

QUESTIONS AND ANSWERS

1. What is the underground church?

Basically, the underground church may be defined as that portion of the Church that prefers to gather in small groups, choosing to meet in homes instead of public buildings. Their services are usually informal, consisting primarily of *koinonia,* prayers, and breaking bread (see Acts 2:42-47; 20:7; 1 Corinthians 14:26). Many of these fellowships regularly hold group discussions rather than always having someone teach.

2. What does "koinonia" mean?

Koinonia has been aptly described as "Body ministry." *Koinonia* is a Greek word usually translated *fellowship* in most translations of the Bible, but it is also rendered "communicate, distribution, contribution, and communion"[1] (see Acts 2:42; Romans 15:26; 1 Corinthians 10:16; 2 Corinthians 9:13; Philemon 1:6). Biblical *koinonia* builds lasting, covenant relationships in believers' lives through genuine *fellowship* with one another and *communion* with God. Each member *contributes* to the common good of the whole. Every member is a minister, *participating* in the daily activities of the church.

3. How does one prepare for persecution and perilous times?

There are at least three things that Christians should do to prepare for the difficult times that are looming upon the horizon. All three are beneficial, so those who take time to prepare are in a win-win situation, regardless of whether they are numbered among those who eventually experience persecution or not.

The first thing one should do is develop a consistent, daily prayer life that includes both prayer and meditation. Prayer is talking to God; meditation is listening. Although it is always important to hear from God, in times of persecution it becomes extremely important. It is also important to learn to interpret your dreams. In Scripture God warned His people of impending calamity through dreams more often than through any other method of communication. He still uses them today.

The second thing to do is become actively involved in the underground church in your area. If there is none, consider seeking God about starting one yourself. The underground church consists of small, covenant, spiritual "families" who faithfully pray for one another and encourage one another in the Lord. Proven covenant relationships are a strong support even in times of peace, but even more so during the perilous times that Paul prophesied would come in these last days (see 2 Timothy 3:1-5).

And last, get out of debt and learn to live within your means. It is also wise to build up a reasonable contingency fund for hard times. Those who follow these three simple steps will be in a much better position to weather whatever the future holds—whether good or bad—than those who foolishly ignore the obvious. The signs are ominous; it is time to prepare. Solomon said, *"He who trusts in his own heart is a fool, but whoever walks wisely will be delivered"* (Proverbs 28:26).

RECOMMENDED READING

Houses That Change the World by Wolfgang Simson. Wolfgang has rightly discerned the transitional mood of this generation and has aptly defined the current structural reformation that is rapidly transforming and redefining "church" as we know it.

ENDNOTE

1. *Strong's Exhaustive Concordance*, Greek #2842.

OTHER BOOKS BY
IRA L. MILLIGAN

Understanding the Dreams You Dream, Volume I:
Biblical Keys for Hearing God's Voice in the Night

God frequently talks through dreams. The Bible reveals that in the past dreams were the most common way God talked to His people. Today's believers often treat dreams like junk mail and throw away the very answers they ask for when they pray for guidance. *Understanding the Dreams You Dream, Volume I* teaches the symbolic language of dreams. Easily understood, this is the ideal reference book for interpreting dreams.

Understanding the Dreams You Dream, Volume II:
Every Dreamer's Handbook

Although numbers are rather common in dreams, most dream books just ignore them. This one doesn't. *Understanding the Dreams You Dream, Volume II* systematically teaches the language of dreams, providing simple solutions to hard questions about dream interpretation.

The Scorpion Within: Revealing the Eight Demonic Roots of Sin

The Scorpion Within is an excellent guide to the root causes of sin and how you can eliminate them to overcome strongholds in your life. It also exposes the demonic influence that satan wields upon humankind. Even longtime believers may be surprised at some activities that put them at risk of demonic control.

Illustrating the Wheel of Nature: Illustrating the Wheel of Nature

"Behold, I give unto you power to tread on serpents and scorpions, and over all the power of the enemy" (Luke 10:19). Most Christians know that *serpents* symbolize demons, but very few know the truth and power that lies hidden in the *scorpion's* symbolism. *The Anatomy of a Scorpion* unveils this mystery and reveals its practical application for every believer. A must for anyone interested in counseling and deliverance (this book is accompanied by a separate counselor's aid— *The Wheel of Nature*).

The Master's Voice: A Practical Guide to Personal Ministry

Some things, like ministering the gifts of the Spirit, are *only* learned from personal experience, but it helps to have a few hints along the way. Both instructional and inspirational, this book intermingles scriptural illustrations and real-life experiences from thirty years of ministry. This book will bless everyone from seasoned veterans to complete novices in spiritual gifts. (This book, titled *La Voz del Maestro*, is also available in Spanish.)

Euroclydon: Illustrating the Four Winds of Heaven

Euroclydon defines and illustrates the four winds of heaven as they oppose the four winds of the earth (see Daniel 7:2; Revelation 7:1). As this ancient conflict unfolds, the role of the prophetic and apostolic ministries in the end-time church is clarified and explained. The restoration of the prophetic and apostolic ministries is part of God's promise to restore all things in Acts 3:21. *Euroclydon* exposes and defines several changes necessary before this promise can be realized.

Rightly Dividing the Word: Unlocking the Hidden Mysteries of the Bible

One of God's favorite tactics is to place truth in plain sight but disguise it as something other than what it is. Almost all spiritual truth is first clothed with a natural disguise. Like wheat, the natural husk must be removed from the grain before it is usable. Moses's Law is spiritual, but it is clothed with various commandments and ordinances that hide its precious truths. *Rightly Dividing the Word* carefully guides the Bible student through the Scriptures to safely obtain spiritual treasures.

Hidden Mysteries of the Bible, Volume I

52 Lesson Foundational Bible Study Course

Hidden Mysteries of the Bible, Volume II

52 Lesson Advanced Bible Study Course

The Hidden Power of Covenant: Releasing
the Fullness of the Blessing of the Gospel of
Jesus Christ

Paul wrote to the church in Rome, *"I know that when I come to you, I shall come in the fullness of the blessing of the gospel of Christ"* (Romans 15:29). What did he know that made him so confident? And what is the *fullness of the blessing of the gospel anyway?* The answers are hidden deep in the mystery of covenant. This book probes and explores this mystery to reveal the surprising answers to these questions.

SERVANT MINISTRIES INC.

To order directly from the internet, go to:

http://servant-ministries.org/

Servant Ministries, Inc.
PO Box 1120
Tioga, LA 71477

IN THE RIGHT HANDS, THIS BOOK WILL CHANGE LIVES!

Most of the people who need this message will not be looking for this book. To change their lives, you need to put a copy of this book in their hands.

> *But others (seeds) fell into good ground, and brought forth fruit, some a hundred-fold, some sixty-fold, some thirty-fold* (Matthew 13:8).

Our ministry is constantly seeking methods to find the good ground, the people who need this anointed message to change their lives. Will you help us reach these people?

> *Remember this—a farmer who plants only a few seeds will get a small crop. But the one who plants generously will get a generous crop* (2 Corinthians 9:6).

**EXTEND THIS MINISTRY BY SOWING
3 BOOKS, 5 BOOKS, 10 BOOKS, OR MORE TODAY,
AND BECOME A LIFE CHANGER!**

Thank you,

Don Nori Sr., Founder
Destiny Image
Since 1982